DISCOVERING THE
HEART OF A MAN

BY

KEN NAIR

3515 E. Onyx Avenue
Phoenix, Arizona 85028

DISCOVERING THE HEART OF A MAN

Discovering the Heart of a Man
© Copyright 1986
By Ken Nair
Printed by Master Printing, Inc.
Phoenix, Arizona
ISBN 0-9615418-5-7

Dedicated to defeating the power of Satan and his influence over the lives of too many unsuspecting Christian men. That we might see more Christian men surrendered to God, illustrating Christ in their daily lives; for their family and others to see and praise God.

With special thanks to my wife Nancy for the hours and hours of typing and retyping until Betty Lou Olmstead came along and did the same thing on her word processor. And, to the following for their dedicated hours of help:

Len Nair	Wayne McKellips
Marilyn Buckner	Janet Smith
Jim Chapman	Cam Tyra
Dannette Withrow	Karen Jansen

TABLE OF CONTENTS

PREFACE

Because this book is meant to be read by people in general, it will be difficult to address specifics. And yet we recognize that any problem is more effectively dealt with when specifically addressed. However, it has been our desire to identify, within the confines of these covers, the "natural inclinations" of the average Christian man as specifically as possible. Still, it will be up to each reader to discover how each principle set forth may or may not apply to his or her own specific circumstances. There is no intention to imply that every man will be identified by every detail within these pages. On the other hand, it would not be wise for a man to reject the testimony of those who, based on their intimate knowledge of him, identify him within these pages.

One does not have to do much marital research to discover that there has been a high degree of misuse and abuse of "authority" in marriages under the guise of "headship of the husband". Too often an unbiblical misrepresentation of authority has been the guideline for many marriages and has even found support in the "church" community. This has caused many Christian women to strongly resent the idea of dependence upon a man: Financially, physically, mentally, emotionally or spiritually. This same irresponsibility on the part of leadership (namely husbands) against wives, in the name of God, has caused some wives to seriously react to the concept that God created woman **for** the man. But I believe that reaction is based on man's misuse of the word "for". There doesn't seem to be an awareness that the word "for" is intended to convey man's inadequacy as a lone being. This book's design is calculated to correct the imbalance in so many marriages that is causing so much distruction.

Wives, when you do see your husband or marriage problems uncovered in this book, why not highlight your findings, for your reference—and your husband's—later on. While reading, please keep in mind also that this book is not meant to draw attention to the condition of a man's physical character but to his spiritual character; not his physical conduct but to his spiritual conduct. When attention is being drawn to physical conduct, it is done so only in order to reveal the condition of the spiritual character.

Wives, the struggles you and your husband face are not against flesh and blood. As Christians, our struggle is against the powers of wickedness and darkness. We trust this book will shed a soul-searching light on those areas that need victory.

Although the illustrations are from real lives and are used with permission, all the names (when necessary) have been changed to conceal identities.

CHAPTER ONE

*HELP MEET ... WHAT'S THAT?

*Often, mistakenly thought to be one word: helpmeet or helpmate. Literally, these words can be read, helper suitable. It may also be expressed, adequate for the purpose designed: helping.

The early years of my life were spent in orphanages. I cannot recall the comfort, joy, or security of being engulf-ed in the arms of a loving father. There is no recollection in my mind of meaningful family relationships between a mother and father nor illustrations of proper godly, hus-band/wife interactions. I am very grateful to God for a twin brother as someone with whom to share life. But even that was difficult because those who oversaw us always tried to keep us separated. The philosophy was that we needed to be separated so that our own personalities could be developed. (Too bad someone didn't let God know that this would be a problem before He allowed multiple births.) I believe that as a result of all this childhood starvation for intimate family relationships, God placed within me a long-ing to have a healthy, fulfilling family.

Eventually I became a Christian and a participant in the life of the church. I started receiving teaching about hus-band/wife roles, father/mother/children relationships and male image concepts. At the time, being newly married, I eagerly embraced these teachings with great expectations. In a few years, we started our family which meant I could apply even more of those teachings in our home.

Had you asked me at that time I would have told you that everything appeared to be going very well. If, as a young Christian, I would have had more supervision or some type of personal accountability things might have been different. But by the time ten years had gone by, my whole family seemed to start falling apart.

At this point, my wife Nancy says that she assessed those negative family relationships and decided that since she had chosen me she would have to put up with me. But the children didn't have a choice in the matter and she couldn't stand by watching me do the same things to them that I was doing to her. I was becoming aware of a very heavy atmosphere of serious alienation in my home.

In spite of my devotion to make diligent application of the teachings I received, all my childhood desires and long-ings for a wholesome marriage and family, were going down the drain! What had happened? Years later, after totally re-evaluating my outlook on the teachings I had received about marriage relationships, I discovered something terribly out of order.

Humanity has been terribly violated by an injustice. A wicked thing has been done to families in general and women in particular! Men have also been seriously cheated. It has all evolved ever so subtly though. This injustice is so common and occurs so frequently that it is not just tolerated, it is almost seen by many people as a necessary part of life. Even though there seems to be signs of an awakening, the "religious community" unfortunately seems to be one of the greatest supporters of this violation. The violation has become so acceptable that it has succeeded in even getting many women to aid in its daily reinforcement.

It is easier to discover the injustice through the senses than through the intellect. As a means of creating an awareness of just how serious this matter is, let me introduce it to you with a question. "Does a woman have either the right or responsibility to question her husband and thus challenge his adequacy as her leader?" Does that question cause your senses to experience turmoil? Many people will react very strongly to that question. The very nature of that question carries with it the implication that women are really almost a human subspecies without the right to question.

And that is the crime . . . thinking that women are inferior to men and need to be controlled!

For this injustice to be corrected, we must go back in time . . . to creation.

Imagine being in God's presence during the creation of our world and watching things take shape that never existed before! You observe some pretty awesome things happen as you watch. As each part of God's handiwork was completed, imagine hearing Him say, "There, that's good . . . I like that," . . . until the creation of man. Then imagine God pausing and saying with great thought, "Ummm . . . no, not good enough, something is missing!" Man, as a lone being, was not thought to be satisfactorily complete in God's mind. So God remedied that situation by creating the complement to man - woman. (Genesis 1 & 2)

It would be impossible for us to determine all of the purposes God had in mind when He created man's complement . . . woman. Of those that are more obvious, one is certain: The purpose of being a "help meet" to man. How many women do you know who have a practical, everyday, working definition for the title or role of help meet?

Women of centuries gone by, being nearer to the events of creation probably had a much clearer picture of what their God-designed purpose was as a help meet in the man/woman relationship. However, over the past centuries I believe the purposes God had in mind when He created woman have been vastly distorted, denied and altered by men. These changes were most likely motivated by man's selfishness in order to suit his own purposes. I also believe that due to these changes, many of the advantages God intended for the man/woman relationship have been lost thus causing much suffering to both! After drawing so much attention to this injustice it's important to recognize that a significant factor contributing to the distortion and violation of God's design and purposes was "the fall" of mankind. A loving relationship between man and woman was not the only thing to suffer as a result of the fall. There was also the separation in the relationship between God and mankind. But all is not lost because God has made provision for the separation between God and man through Jesus Christ. God has provided further help for mankind in rebuilding the relationship between God and man by sending us the Holy Spirit. This whole process is known as Salvation. Its design includes bringing about the **regeneration of our spirit** through the entrance of God's Holy Spirit. The person whom we were before salvation and therefore unable to identify with God, is supposed to become a new and different person totally surrendered to God. This means Christ is to become **Lord of our lives** as well as Savior, inabling us to experience a new God-like reflection on our marriage.

Looking at the Christian marriage relationship with that

regeneration in mind, there is no excuse for living our lives in the same manner as the old unregenerated man and acting towards our wife in an unGodly/unChrist-like way. I think the divorce rate, even among Christians, shows that the Christian community at large is illustrating this same immaturity or lack of understanding of God's concepts. It is as though no regeneration took place at all. Men are still reflecting on husband/wife relationships with the same lack of esteem towards women that they had before salvation. The divorce statistics seem to reflect that there's no "life-giving" difference in too many Christian marriages. Yielding to God's ways brings life, not (divorce) death! Our spiritual ignorance about God's ways is robbing us of our joy in marriage. Even more serious though, it is robbing us of a deeper relationship with God which can only come through a higher degree of godliness or spiritual maturity. A **loving** husband/wife relationship requires a high degree of spiritual maturity or a more God-like understanding. This seems to be missing in so many marriages within the Christian community.

> *"A new commandment I give you: Love one another,* **as I have loved you,** *so you* **must love** *one another."* *(John 13:34 N.I.V.) "If anyone loves me, he will obey my teaching. My Father will love him, and we will come to him and make our home with him. He who does not love Me will not obey my teaching.* **These words** *you hear* **are not My own, they belong to the Father** *who sent me." (John 14:23, 24 N.I.V.) "Dear friends, let us love one another, for love comes from God. Everyone who loves has been born of God and knows God.* **Whoever does not love does not know God,** *because God is love." (John 4:7, 8 N.I.V.) "Since by your obedience to the Truth through the Holy Spirit you have purified your hearts for the sincere affection of the brethren, see that you* **love one another fervently** *from a pure heart." (I Peter 1:22 AMP. Bible)*

We see revealed in the following, further evidence of

man's departure from God's concepts with regards to the design of woman. Although God's thinking during the process of creation was that man's full value would not be completely realized until **after** the creation of woman, men (Christian or otherwise) do not always attach the same high degree of importance and regard for womankind as God does. It is unscriptural and improper for Christians to place less value on God's creation, in this case women, than God does. We should place great value on **all** of God's creation. I'm not saying we should value any negative traits a woman or anyone might have. We should, however, value women as a creation of God to such an extent that our first response if we see a negative trait is not, "Aha, see how sinful you are!" Rather, the response should be, "because you are worth caring for, this negative makes me aware that you are struggling and I wonder how I may serve God by serving you through finding a solution." In actuality, many men tend to focus on negatives in women while overlooking their own negatives. Those men demonstrate an attitude of superiority which says in essence, "**Men** are quite sufficient because they do not need overseers like women do." As a result those same men feel that this "male sufficiency" is what qualifies them to be the custodians of women. This attitude is generally not intentional, but rather the by-product of **instinctive** selfishness. Ephesians 5:28 addressed the issue of the selfishness in men: Men, use that **love of self** as a guideline for how much to love your wives.

Too many women are also carrying around very negative attitudes about themselves. I believe these adverse feelings are generally developed by the powerful influence of negative words, actions and attitudes (especially those expressed non-verbally) towards women by the men in their lives.

There is a **very strong** need in women to be acceptable to their leaders. That need is so strong that it will make them very alert to indications of possible rejection. A woman's need to **not** experience rejection, especially from father or husband, will powerfully influence the conclusions she may draw about herself for her entire life. Improperly valuing women, which often begins when they are little girls, will cause them to develop many negative perspectives about their own self-worth. Women will often conclude that they are actually reject material. All these negative attitudes (in men and in women towards women) have hindered the capacity of women to fulfill the roles for which God created them. Some drastic re-evaluations need to take place in the minds of men and women before these devaluing attitudes toward women can change.

I'm convinced that the steps required before mankind can again reflect upon women from God's perspective must be taken first by men. God desires that all Christian husbands have righteous attitudes toward the male/female relationship. Yet there seems to be a "log jam" when it comes to developing the necessary spiritual maturity which would allow them to see their wives from God's perspective. Here is the "log jam": If a man does not know what a righteous, God-centered relationship is, it's natural to conclude that he is spiritually immature and lacks relationship skills. Consequently he **will** be blind and unable to see his unrighteous/ungodly attitudes. That same immaturity will prevent him from **even realizing** that he should seek help. Without help the problem continues. Sounds like a never ending circle doesn't it? However, there are those who are seeking direction.

It has been a great source of joy to be involved in a ministry of helping couples see some significant scriptural principles about husband/wife relationships. We have determined that there is a special need in the Christian community for men to receive training about spiritual leadership. Furthermore we feel that those wives whose husbands have joined our relationship workshops are wives who have very special husbands with a very unusual, high degree of commitment to their marriages. Those men are willing to be examined as to whether or not they are illustrating Christ in their daily lives. As we have worked with these husbands discipling them toward more Christ-likeness, many of their wives have asked, "How can I more effectively assist my husband in his quest for Christ-likeness?"

That question is actually illustrating the need to understand what the role of being a help meet involves. Over the years I have been asking women if they could give me a description of that God-ordained, vocational word. As of yet I have not received a clear, practical, everyday, usable definition. So let's take the time here to give a definition to the term, "help meet." In order to do that we will have to go back again to the beginning of creation.

First, let's simplify the word "help meet," to "helper." Now reflect with me on Genesis 2:18. Here we observe God creating man's complement and in her name, Helper, expressing the purpose for her creation. Contrary to some popular notions, this term does not mean servant or slave, nor does it have any implications that would allow her to be thought of as an inferior product. In fact the words used in Genesis reveal that God was satisfied that what he had created was quite adequate. God said, "He created a helper **suitable** for him (the man)."

God's perspective was that she would complete him; she would be the completion of that which was missing before the creation of woman. Therefore, as far as man is concerned, I believe a woman is meant to be God's expression of balance. As a part of that balance, a woman's design then would be to help her husband see life from an altogether different perspective. She could be a means through which he could expand his outlook on life. She would be a source of joy to him too; providing him with one of the most meaningful companionships ever possible between two human beings. A man with a wife would also be free from the pressures of having to make the decisions of life alone. But more important than anything else a wife could be a reflector through whom he examines his ability to portray Christ **to her.**

However, the fear of being rejected by her husband makes it very difficult for a woman to make herself want to risk being so vulnerable. The fear of the consequences of honestly expressing herself in all the areas of their relationship, sharing her concerns, ideas, dreams and (especially) her feelings can make her very hesitant. Therefore, to help provide motivation, a wife will need to have a spiritual guideline; a practical, everyday, definition of the term helper. May we suggest the following definition to meet that need.

"Being so committed to godliness in their marriage as to risk the safety of self protection; not giving in to the fear of being vulnerable while constructively and precisely sharing even the inner-most feelings of her heart. Honestly expressing her appraisal of their relationship, positive or negative, so that her husband can truly live with her in an understanding way, caring for her as Christ does." Even though that kind of honesty might cause her to sometimes feel unsafe, a wife must purpose to be responsible and answerable to God's call and always honor her husband with constructive honesty.

This definition may cause many women to recognize a need to totally re-evaluate their role as a wife. While you have been reading you may have begun to consider the need to change your thinking about marriage relationships. You may also discover a new desire to become a better "help meet" to your husband. With that in mind, there are five very important questions that must be asked as a first step towards correcting improper thinking about marriage relationships. Please take the time to seriously think through and answer these questions:

1. Would your husband be more acceptable to you if you could:
   A. Make your husband into the person **you want** him to be, or
   B. see him become the person **God wants** him to be?
      A. ☐   B. ☐

2. Would you be more satisfied in life if your husband:
   A. Provided for you that which **you want from** him, or
   B. provided that which **God wants** him to provide **for** you?
      A. ☐   B. ☐

3. Do you have any preconceived, worldly, unscriptural goals or ideas about what success in life is and is your

purpose to get him to **help you** achieve those goals?
Yes ☐   No ☐

4. Is it more important to you that your husband become the kind of man that:

A. Causes **others to think** he is a "real man," or

B. the man God wants him to be: Christ-like?

A. ☐   B. ☐

5. Do you need to re-evaluate what you might be expecting from life as well as from your Christian husband in light of God's value system?

Yes ☐   No ☐

These questions are designed to reveal improper relationship perspectives that can be harmful to God's design for marriages. But these are not the only things we want to examine. Since the goal of this book is to help women understand men, let's reflect now on the role of the husband.

The word "husband" in the biblical sense means overseer; responsible leader. To be a **responsible spiritual leader** a man's own relationship with God must be his **central** concern. Only then can a man become more responsible and Christ-like. We know that God said of Christ, "This is my beloved Son, in whom I am well pleased," so if we become Christ-like then God will be pleased with us, too! As a man seeks to become more Christ-like, he could ask himself this question, "Are my words, actions, and attitudes towards my wife pleasing to God?"

To further examine God's design and a man's relationship with Him we must again go back to the Old Testament.

As we examine Genesis 1:26 and 3:16, we see that, in the beginning, God created man and identified him as the ruler. However the term ruler does not mean dominator. Instead it means that as a husband he is being asked to be a representative of God's authority; administering to his wife responsibly, as God would. A Christian husband should illustrate the attributes of God: Love, patience, peace, joy, always forgiving, very available, and definitely understanding. Conducting himself in a manner that gains and maintains his wife's trust. Proving that he has a strong commitment to be obedient to God as the leader of his wife's spirit.

Although the term "spiritual leader" is one that is heard frequently in the Christian community, it doesn't seem to have a practical, everyday, definition. The three most common expressions I've heard people use to describe a spiritual leader are as follows:

First, a man who really knows the Bible or has memorized a lot of Scripture. That should be a vital part of every Christian's activities, but it won't make a man a spiritual leader. My Bible shows me that Satan knows Scripture and I sure wouldn't want him to be my example of spiritual leadership.

Second, I've also heard it said that a man who is a powerful or charismatic speaker is a good spiritual leader. But then, doesn't that mean that the average husband, who is neither, might never qualify as a spiritual leader?

Third, the most common, is described as the man who has his family "in line"; "under his thumb" ...

May I propose that none of these qualify a man as a spiritual leader! Let me give my definition of a spiritual leader:

"A man who has the ability to perceive his wife's spirit (her inner-person), understand its need and know how to care for that need. He then will be able and ready to serve God by ministering to his wife's spirit in a manner that would cause her to grow more and more spiritually mature." A husband should want his wife to be able to come to him with any concern, anytime, and have her feel in her spirit that he cares for her. All of this is a very difficult task for a man, but he is obligated before God to accept that challenge when he accepts the role of being a husband.

Interestingly enough, most men don't have a clue that the concept just mentioned is a part of what God requires of them. They are blind, unable to see what is necessary for the marriage relationship. Because of their own spiritual immaturity, they are unable to care for the spirit of their wife.

But most wives usually are **not** blind to the lack of spiritual maturity or the poor relationship skills exhibited by their husband. Because a wife does recognize the damage that is taking place in her marriage relationship she will usually begin to share her concerns with her husband. It is not unusual for a husband to be very unresponsive to his wife's cautions or not value her suggestions for solutions. This is especially true if he **is blind** to the fact that there are indeed problems in his marriage. His lack of godly understanding will block his ability to comprehend and respond skillfully. The result will be an inability to provide godly leadership. A wife needs the type of spiritual leadership that will assist her in her own quest for a greater degree of spiritual maturity. So now they are both negatively affected by his spiritual immaturity or lack of relationship skills. They certainly are not experiencing the greater joys of a God-centered marriage relationship.

The rate of divorce in the world proves to me that there is a severe lack of spiritual leadership skills in men. Why else would multiplied marriages continue down the path of destruction if men were, in fact, providing **effective** leadership. To an even greater degree then, we see the evidence that proves there is a definite need in the world for more men who are willing to accept the challenge of a stronger, more intense commitment to God to become more and more like Christ. Men who would challenge themselves to overcome the suspicious nature towards women, which is so natural to men. Purposing to defeat their masculine pride with its accompanying negative outlook. Men who would dare to let their wives have the chance to evaluate them. Giving their wives the freedom of expressing whether or not they think their husbands are becoming more and more an example of Christ-likeness. Scripture labels those men who are willing to have their lives critiqued, as **wise**. (Proberbs 9:8,9).

The reason I made the preceding challenge to men, is

because I am firmly convinced that part of God's design, especially concerning the purposes of a Christian wife, includes the following: A husband can use the condition of his wife's emotions and spirit as a means of effectively measuring his success at being the leader of her spirit; that is, has he cared for her as Christ would? A husband would be able to determine then if he was exchanging his natural ungodly, worldly, human ways for Christ-likeness through his wife's responses to him. Here is another way of stating this concept: "If a husband is conducting himself in his marriage the way that God prescribes he should, it can be verified through the stability of his wife's spiritual and emotional condition." This is what scripture says:

> "Husbands, love your wives, just as Christ also loved the church and gave Himself up for her, that He might sanctify her, having cleansed her by the washing of water with the word, that He might present to Himself the church in all her glory, having no spot or wrinkle or any such thing; but that she should be holy and blameless. So husbands ought also to love their own wives as their own bodies. He who loves his wife loves himself; for no one ever hated his own flesh, but nourishes and cherishes it, just as Christ also does the church." (Ephesians 5:25-29 NAS)

The command that a Christian become more Christ-like requires that a man learn to deal with three major problem areas which will cause a separation in his relationship with God and his wife. (I John and James 1:14, 15):

1. Immorality - lust of the flesh - yielding to the desires of the body.
2. Selfishness - lust of the eyes - yielding to the dictates of the mind.
3. Ego - pride of life - yielding to the immaturity of our spirit.

If these problem areas have a place in a man's heart they will greatly hinder his relationship with God and his ability

to be influenced by the Holy Spirit. This will result in a
limitation on the Holy Spirit's freedom to guide and protect him. Consequently, everything for which a man is
responsible will be negatively affected.

> *"Those who live according to their sinful nature have
> their minds set on what that nature desires; but
> those who live in accordance with the Spirit have
> their minds set on what the Spirit desires. The mind
> of the sinful man is death, but the mind controlled
> by the Spirit is life and peace, because the sinful
> mind is hostile to God. It does not submit to God's
> law, nor can it do so. Those controlled by their sin-
> ful nature cannot please God. You, however, are
> controlled not by your sinful nature but by the Spirit,
> if the Spirit of God lives in you. And if anyone does
> not have the Spirit of Christ, he does not belong to
> Christ. But if Christ is in you, your body is dead
> because of sin, yet your spirit is alive because of
> rightousness. And if the Spirit of him who raised
> Jesus from the dead is living in you, he who raised
> Christ from the dead will also give life to your mor-
> tal bodies through his Spirit, who lives in you.
> Therefore, brothers, we have an obligation - but it
> is not to our sinful nature, to live according to it.
> For if you live according to the sinful nature, you
> will die; but if by the Spirit you put to death the
> misdeeds of the body, you will live. Those who are
> led by the Spirit of God are the sons of God."*
> *(Romans 8:5-14 N.I.V.)*

   In summary, isn't it encouraging to discover that the role
of a help meet is one of great honor? That a woman does
not have to reflect on herself as an inferior product. She
does not have to reflect upon herself as one not worthy
to have her dreams about a meaningful relationship ever
fulfilled.
   Before moving on, let me give some words of caution.
You may find that you can identify so strongly with what
is written within these pages that many emotions that

you've tried to deny or ignore may be revived. Please be careful as you deal with those emotions to avoid impulsively drawing the simple conclusion that, "he is to blame for **all** of the grief in my life!"

Our goal should not simply be that of placing blame, but to develop understanding so God's solutions can be applied and the resulting benefits experienced. As you read on, ask God to give you compassion towards all those for whom He has sent His Son to die, especially your husband. Realizing that many husbands still are not experiencing all of the benefits that life, as God designed it, has to offer.

CHAPTER TWO

IF MEN THINK MORE LIKE GOD, WILL THEY UNDERSTAND WOMEN?

When it comes to relationships, many men have complained that they are not very creative thinkers. This makes me realize that I'm not alone when I say it's difficult for me to think of unique ways to express to my family how much they mean to me. (Even so, difficulty is no excuse for not trying.) You can imagine how satisfied I was with myself when not too long ago a creative idea did occur to me. It happened while talking with Mike, a friend of mine who is an announcer on a local Christian radio station. I wondered if my request would be out of line, so it was with some hesitation that I asked Mike this question. "Are you ever able to make personal comments or announcements on the radio?" His reply was comforting, "I sure can! Why? Did you have something in mind?" I expressed my wish that he could mention my wife's name (Nancy) and each of my children, letting them know how special they are to me and that I love them very much. Mike graciously accepted my request and we established 7:35 the next morning as "the" time; he would do it right after the 7:30 commercials. With a sense of inner pleasure I asked each member of my family to be sure and tune in to Mike's radio program the next morning at 7:30 AM. Each one wanted to know why, but I said, "you'll just have to tune in and listen. It's a special announcement."

The next morning I tried to act very calm although inside I was really excited about their hearing my special attempt to communicate my love to them. My radio was tuned in the night before. At 7:30 we heard Mike say, "Right after these messages, stay tuned for a special announcement." Then at 7:35, Mike surpassed my expectations as he made the announcement. He could have merely said, "Hey Nancy, Denise, Kristy and Sarah, your dad loves you!" But he didn't. He started off by telling about a friend of his named Ken Nair; how we became acquainted; the ministry I'm involved in and what it meant to him. Then he described my family by name and expressed my desire to let them know how special they are to me and that I loved each one of them.

How grateful I was to him for so effectively communicating my feelings for them. You can imagine my disappointment, though, when one of my daughters who wasn't living at home missed it completely. My message didn't get communicated to her because she wasn't tuned in! I wanted to let her know that I loved her, too, and it didn't happen. You see, I know that **constantly** ministering to relationships is **very** important.

Marriage relationships are like that too; they need to be ministered to constantly. In evaluating how to minister to the needs of today's relationships, I have noticed that one of the most persistent problems between husbands and wives is their inability to communicate. I don't mean that no verbal communication is taking place. I do mean there are **wide gaps** in the **understanding** between husbands and wives about what each other means when he or she is talking. Messages between husbands and wives are not being received from one another because they are not "tuned in" to each other. Not only are husbands and wives not tuned in to each other, often they aren't even on the same "wave-length." Generally the blame for this problem is laid at the feet of wives with statements from husbands like, "No, no, that's not what I said. Don't **you** get anything right?!" But my Bible says that the burden for making sure proper communications are taking place rests on the husband's shoulders. It **is** the **husband's** responsibility for making sure that they **both** are tuned in on the same "wave-length." *(I Peter 3:7. A* **husband** *is to live with his wife in an understanding way.)* I believe the average woman is more naturally able to understand the requirements of a relationship. Therefore, she probably will have to initiate a lot of the pathfinding until her husband understands how to carry out his responsibilities. One of the things that helps a wife be a pathfinder; assisting her as she trys to locate and tune in on her husband's "wave-length", is to give her some basic facts about men. We will get to those facts in just a moment.

> Please keep in mind as
> you read each chapter
> that the facts being dealt
> with, in regard to the
> nature of men, are not
> necessarily covered in
> order of importance.

Before moving on, let me emphasize the destructiveness of this problem area: The problem is confused communication between men and women. It is like the disease of cancer; unless cured, it grows worse and worse until it kills. **First,** there is the natural **in**ability in men to understand women. **Second,** that inability usually leads to arguments or fights. **Third,** arguing and fighting has the effect of killing the desire in either or both to even want to talk together. Communication problems between men and women are usually more stressful on women because they are usually more emotional. They will usually react **more visibly** to disharmony. Unfortunately the most common conclusion people draw because of these emotional outbursts, is that women's emotions **are** the problem. This notion is reinforced with the following: Most men willingly admit that they don't understand a woman's emotions and are not emotionally inclined and yet, even without this understanding they readily accept the title of leader in the marriage. And too often in the minds of men this is the formula for leadership: Leaders are supposed to take charge and everyone knows that the people in charge are the one's who decide how to care for those in their charge—finding solutions for problems. Most men think that because they're supposed to be the leader, that that makes **their** solutions automatically the **right** solutions. Therefore their solution to the conflicts between husbands and wives is that, if women weren't so independent, strong-willed and un-submissive there wouldn't be any problems in marriages! This erroneous thinking then, causes many men to conclude that the **main** struggle they face in their relationships is their wives. On the contrary, the greatest struggles a man will face in his marriage is not those struggles he will have with his wife, but the struggles he will have with God over obedience. Will he be obedient to God concerning the responsibilities God has given him as a Christian husband? Marriage can and often does, have the ability to reveal one's secret self. It can be a magnifying glass through which God can identify for a husband whether or not he specifically understands God's formula for a successful marriage relationship in specific situations. A man could choose to gauge his adaquacy as a husband by the condition of his marriage. Does he have the ability to successfully care for his marriage? Does he understand and know how to apply God's concepts for this relationship?

As you read, there is a definite need to keep in mind that just because a man may be a Christian, we cannot automatically conclude that he knows about (or as illustrated in too many cases even cares about) positively responding to God's will for his marriage. And even though he has been given the responsibility by God to be his wife's spiritual leader, too often it seems as though the average man is not willing to discipline himself as he should to apply what he does know to be God's ways. The Bible says it this way, "No one understands - no one intelligently discerns or comprehends: no one seeks out God." (Romans 3:11 AMP Bible)

Many women find themselves drawing the conclusion that most men are dead set against marriage and could care less about having a good relationship **with** their wives. That conclusion is drawn because most women do not have an awareness of some basic facts about men. Remember, as a wife, if your goal is to be a help meet in the truest sense, you must acquire an understanding about some basic facts which reveal the condition of a man's heart. You must grasp as a reality that men operate on a **different** wave-length than women. In order to help him tune in to you, you must become aware of the wave-length on which the natural man is actually operating. Let's reveal the **first** basic fact about how many men operate, in this chapter. We will address other basic facts in subsequent chapters.

FACT #1 . . . **When it comes to being a truly Christian husband, most men honestly are not aware that there is a difference between their own ideals and those concepts set forth by God.**

> *"My thoughts are not your thoughts, neither are your ways my ways, declares the Lord." (Isaiah 55:8)*

Scripture reveals that the natural state of man's heart is in direct contrast to God's heart. Too often it is assumed that a Christian man does know what is required of him as a Christian husband. That's very seldom true. Nor is it often true that a Christian man will, without hesitation, be respectful enough of God to obey what he does know to be God's commands. Therefore, as a disobedient child of God, he may need to be corrected. That's one of the functions of the Holy Spirit, to bring conviction, and sometimes chastening for repentance, to Christians for violating God's ways.

> *"And when He comes He will convict and convince the world and bring demonstration to it about sin and about righteousness—uprightness of heart and right standing with God—and about judgements." (John 16:8 AMP. Bible)*
>
> *"My son, despise not thou the chastening of the Lord, nor faint when thou are rebuked of him: For whom the Lord loveth he chasteneth, and scourgeth every son whom he receiveth. If ye endure chastening, God dealeth with you as with sons; for what son is he whom the father chasteneth not? But if ye be without chastisement, wherof all are partakers, then ye are bastards, and not sons. Furthermore we have had fathers of our flesh which corrected us, and we gave them reverence: shall we not much rather be in subjection unto the Father of spirits, and live? For they verily for a few days chastened us after their*

*own pleasure; but he for our profit, that we might
be partakers of his holiness. Now no chastening for
the present seemeth to be joyous, but grievous:
nevertheless afterward it yieldeth the peaceable fruit
of righteousness unto them which are excercised
thereby." (Hebrews 12:5b-11 KJV)*

The Holy Spirit desires to prompt us to repentance and
to see us come to the point of humbly acknowledging our
wrongs and seeking to be instructed in righteousness. That
being the case, couldn't the Holy Spirit use a wife's feelings of estrangement to point out a husband's unChrist-
like ways? Couldn't a wife be one whom God might use
to help her husband see that he is not acting according
to God's word? A man's greatest freedom is exercised when
he can **challenge himself** with the possibility that God is
using his wife to confront him. Nevertheless, the bondage
of pride may prompt a man to react negatively when confronted with his unChrist-like ways, especially if the confronting is through his wife. He may become angry, stub-
born, or very resentful towards his wife.

Complications and difficulties usually begin early in marriage relationships. For example, let's say you know a young
couple and the young man does not know what God ex-
pects of him. However, this young man's future wife has
specifically visualized all the ways that he is going to fulfill
all her dreams now, and in the future. Consider the potential troubles in store for a woman if she develops all of those
specific images in her mind about what her marriage and
her husband **will be.** Especially since almost every man will
readily admit that he doesn't have the faintest idea how
women think. The chances of any man being the perfect
husband (actually understanding his wife's dreams and then
fulfilling all of them) are pretty slim. If your reasons for getting married were like this young lady's then please consider the following:

• Maybe the dreams you've developed in your mind
about what the ideal marriage is, are ideals that do
not line up with God's blueprints.

- Maybe you were looking for a knight in shining armor to help you escape the harsh realities of your present life. If so, your reasons for getting married to this man were not praiseworthy reasons. A premarriage 'escape' mentality will severely hinder the building of a good marriage relationship.

- Maybe you thought your pre-marriage life was boring and you got married to add spice to your life.

If you find that you have used the above reasons it would indicate that you hadn't learned how to handle facing life as it really was and marriage is no place to try and hide from life! These and many more faulty reasons are poor motivation for marriage and will only complicate the relationship.

It's possible that the man you married doesn't have a clear working knowledge of those purposes that the Designer of marriage had in mind when He designed marriages. This is typical of most men. It is even less likely, then, that the average man is going to be able to fulfill those needs created by dreams that are faulty.

Being inadequate when it comes to godliness is natural to men, but those human inadequacies are even further amplified when they are passed on from generation to generation.

".... God visits the sins of the father upon the children unto the third and fourth generation ....."
(Exodus 20:5 KJV)

Still, we are not without hope. Psalm 119:9 through 11 says a man can keep his ways pure (God centered) by vigorously searching the Scriptures. He will more effectively avoid offending God by making God's ways **his** ways and letting **the Bible's message become a part of his inner-most being** and character. If **men** would have been faithful throughout the centuries in their pursuit of godliness, they would have been instructing their children daily. Their children would have been taught daily, through examples of God's methods for successful marriage relationships.

Men would have been prepared from childhood to become the husband's God intended them to be. In their own homes children would have witnessed their fathers illustrating through personal examples, loving, tender, godly attitudes towards their mothers. Fathers would have been teaching their sons through personal example how to highly value a wife, how to patiently listen to her opinions and give her feelings serious consideration. They would have shown their sons what it means to live with a wife in an understanding way.

" . . . . . *the father to the children shall make known thy truth.*" *(Isaiah 38:19b KJV)*

And God commanded Moses to instruct the men; who were supposed to be the governors of their families . . . "*and these words I am commanding you this day, shall be* **first** *in your own mind and heart; then you shall whet and sharpen them, also as to make them penetrate and teach and impress them diligently upon the minds and hearts of your children, and you shall talk of them when you sit in your house, and when you walk by the way, and when you lie down and when you rise up.*" *(Deuteronomy 6:6,7 AMP. Bible)*

Although your husband may not have had day-by-day, situation-by-situation training as a boy, all is not lost! God has made additional provisions for the need in a husband to understand his wife through a very valuable source of "on the job" training. That provision is through you, his wife! Ephesians 5:25 reveals that a husband can determine through his wife how well he is or is not illustrating Christ.

If your husband is willing to learn about God's requirements of him as a Christian husband, you must then, as his God-ordained helper seriously consider your responsibility to help him learn. Along with that responsibility you should also recognize and accept the following unavoidable fact: Even though you've both committed yourselves to and are intently working on building your marriage . . . trials and pressures will still find their way into your lives. You will discover that even with the best of intentions you are still going to offend each other. There are no problem-free marriages. Two people living together are going to experience friction with each other. So don't let Satan accuse you and make you feel as though you are failing just because you are experiencing rough times. As a means of reinforcement, tell one another daily of your commitment to God and each other. You can count on having your commitment to each other tested often by that one who has been so suitably named, the destroyer!

Here again we are faced with a possible misunderstanding. It's easy to tell a wife to forget some offenses or leave some problems unsolved because they seem too "nit-picky" to deal with. It may appear at times as though struggles between a husband and wife are nothing more than a passing disagreement or an insignificant fight between them. However, nothing is insignificant to God when it comes to watching over his children. Through this simple relationship difficulty, God may be letting this husband see his capacity to illustrate Christ-likeness or reveal to him his unChrist-like responses.

In our workshops, we see many husbands making commitments to become more and more Christ-like. In anticipation of what lies ahead, we try to prepare those husbands for the struggles and emotionally painful experiences that they will face. The process wherein we men learn how to lay down our lives for our wives can be emotionally very painful, and Satan would like to take advantage of our human weaknesses by convincing us that all our efforts are worthless. Satan wants us to grow weary and give up. Often Satan will tempt us to give up or become disobedient to God through some very well-meaning people. Those people may let us know that **they** don't want to see us hurt. **They** don't believe that God wants anyone to ever hurt. But the New Testament is filled with reminders that suffering is a part of our calling. In addition, I'm convinced that before we can meaningfully minister to others we must personally experience a type of suffering in our own lives which will allow us to **effectively identify with others and** relate to their suffering. If it is God's desire that a man develop the capacity to identify with those who are hurting; those who are heart-broken, or emotionally grieved (and I believe it is - see Hebrews 2:10), then each man will himself also have to experience similar grief.

While experiencing the emotional suffering brought on by dying to self, it will benefit a husband greatly if he will focus on two things.

First, he must allow those emotional hurts to prove to him that a person's spirit (inner person) can actually suffer and hurt.

Second, he must add to that awareness the understanding that unChrist-like ways, in any relationship, will definitely produce negative emotional effects. Remembering those two things will enable him to more effectively minister in the Lord's behalf, since he is learning to identify with the spirit of others by experiencing similar hurts. The pain of dying to self will both help him know first-hand how others feel when they are hurting and motivate him to stop being the source of others hurting. He can then minister to them with more understanding and compassion. That's part of God's plan.

> "Praise be to the God and Father of our Lord Jesus Christ, the father of compassion and the God of all comfort, who comforts us in all our troubles, so that we can comfort those in any trouble with the comfort we ourselves have received from God. For just as the sufferings of Christ flow over into our lives, so also through Christ our comfort and salvation; if we are comforted, it is for your comfort, which produces in you patient endurance of the same sufferings we suffer." (II Corinthians 1:3-6 N.I.V.)

It's very common to see a wife who knows that her husband is experiencing some heavy pressures in life and see her want to do more than just stand by and watch. Some of those wives will want to find relief for their husbands. That kindheartedness is commendable, but a wife must first concern herself with this question: Does God want her to assume the responsibility of relieving her husband of pressures? Since God is aware of what is happening in our lives, it is possible that she may be interfering with God's design. God's intentions are that trials be used to strengthen a man as he learns to conquer them or to cause a man to examine attitudes he may have towards God or those trials.

> I make a distinction between the wife who is trying to **warn** her husband of potential trials, pressures, or problems (which I think is proper and within God's design) and the wife who is trying to **keep** her husband from going through trials, pressures or problems. Or she might even be attempting to keep him from experiencing the consequences of disobedience. Warnings are appropriate, but trying to eliminate trials or barricade her husband from life's struggles, I believe, is incorrect.

There are some almost unbelievably cruel circumstances taking place in more marriages than is generally known— even in some "nice" families. And cruelty cannot be measured by a given standard. What may be extremely cruel to one person may only be uncomfortable to another; what may be cruel to one may be inhuman to another. So, keeping in mind the idea of emotional suffering, it's not unusual to see some wives who have been so deeply hurt physically and/or emotionally by their husbands in the past that they enjoy seeing him go through anything that brings him grief or torment. These wives have decided that their husband's proper reward in life is for him to suffer. It has become a source of joy for those wives to see their husbands experience the same kind of agony that he has caused them.

Let's say we discover a wife who wants that type of revenge but we add the following positive factor to her situation. Her husband recognizes that he has been offensive, he recognizes how ungodly his ways have been and he has decided to change. He wants to see his character change and hostilities stop. However, his wife, who has suffered for years, is not ready to dismiss his offenses so quickly. She still wants to see him suffer and pay for the hurt he has caused her.

This kind of situation is much more common than might be imagined. I know of many cases where wives have been literally praying that their husbands would die on their jobs or get killed on the freeway while driving home, etc. And you'd be surprised at how many of those husbands **don't have a clue** that their wives harbored that kind of violent hostility towards them! That's why we must address the following issue.

There already are too many people hurting unnecessarily in the world. They are suffering because they have not been able to experience life as God has designed it. **As a wife,** you may be one of life's casualties, having been deeply hurt. But maybe your husband realizes that he has been out-of-line and has purposed to God that he will change. However, you refuse to let go of your bitter, vengeful attitudes. God is telling your heart to forgive him but you refuse. You do not want to join your husband in rebuilding your marriage. You refuse to see anything in your husband worth salvaging. Even though God is speaking to your heart, you let those bitter/vengeful attitudes separate you from God. You are making yourself a friend of Satan, if you purposefully give up, resist, or shirk your God-given responsibility to assist your husband in making your marriage Christ-centered. Let me warn you of something you will find happening to you—something that you did not expect. You will start developing the very characteristics in your personality that you hated in your husband. I have watched that happen over and over again without exception.

Shortly, we will use two columns to indicate two different attitudes. The **left** column sets forth **Christ-like attitudes** and the **right** column sets forth **wrong attitudes.** Many times a Christian wife is able to see herself in the left column until she gives up on her role and purposes to stop helping her husband while he tries to rebuild the marriage. Too often, a defeated, destroyed wife, reduced to "getting-out-for-survival," is precisely what it takes to finally make a man realize he had better become concerned and do something. Having brought his marriage to disaster by devastating his wife, many a husband will finally recognize his folly and decide that he had better start trying to rebuild the relationship. Still, if a husband is really trying to restore his marriage and his wife throws away her *God-ordained responsibility to be her husband's help meet, she seems to switch columns and exchange the positive characteristics for the negative characteristics. Her character actually changes and she becomes the offensive person she resented him for being. Perhaps in the past you were the only one who cared about the condition of your marriage. Maybe it was you who illustrated the positive characteristics in the left column. In the past was it your husband who regularly illustrated the negative characteristics in the right column? Is it your husband who is now trying to develop the positive characteristics shown in the left-hand column? Is it possible to see yourself in the right-hand column now?

The boxes are provided so that you can mark them. Those characteristics which you feel are a part of your life please mark with a ⬚W for wife. Those characteristics which you feel your husband illustrates please mark with an ⬚H for husband.

---

*Don't forget the grief that came to Esau when he disrespected God's requirements. (Genesis 25:27-34, 27:1-44)

Characteristics that **illustrate a Christ-like love:**	Characteristics that **illustrate a lack of Christ-like love:**
☐ wants a good relationship and is motivated to do that which will gain partner's acceptance and approval.	☐ is uninterested in partner's efforts to keep peace or gain reconciliation.
☐ is genuinely concerned about the effects of marriage conflicts on their children.	☐ is selfishly motivated for own interests. Redefines "what is right or even scriptural" to suit self. If children are being negatively affected this spouse says their wrong is right ... because their wrong actions are supposedly motivated by what is "best" for the children, even though it is destroying the family.
☐ is trying to be cautious in conversation. Desires to say only the right thing. Fears saying the wrong thing. Maybe even talks seldom to avoid making mistakes.	☐ is making partner feel incompetent, says their cautiousness is awkward stupidity.

☐ while hurting, still wants harmony and attempts to reach out for comfort from partner.	☐ ignores hurting partner. Makes them feel unacceptable. Conveys the detached attitude, "If I need anything from you, I'll let you know."
☐ tries to do thoughtful things to build relationship.	☐ rejects thoughtfulness and says, "You're just trying to manipulate me."
☐ seeks counsel for corrective steps when mistakes are made.	☐ continues to blame spouse for all the mistakes. Takes advantage of partner's willingness to bend over backwards for solutions.
☐ hopes things will improve.	☐ is never satisfied with any type of progress. Makes partner feel that he or she can never do anything right.
☐ tries to humble self.	☐ talks abusively, wants to humiliate spouse.
☐ is emotionally affected by broken relationship.	☐ ridicules partner as an emotionally weak person.

☐ examines self for ways to improve.	☐ increases faultfinding, looks at partner with critical eyes. Neglects to examine own need for doing right.
☐ wants to demonstrate marital loyalty (even though there may have been personal failures in the past). wants to build togetherness.	☐ gives affections to others. Tries to excuse any wrong by pointing out partners past failures. Makes partner feel repulsed. Has an independent spirit of, "Who needs you?"
☐ sees value in, and the need for building a commitment to one another.	☐ says, "I missed out on life because of you!" Wants to "taste" more of life now, outside of marriage.
☐ seeks to develop friendships with those who have higher standards and will assist with goals of becoming more Christ-like.	☐ develops friendships with others who do not care about lowered standards of conduct. Seeks friendships with those whom they accused in the past of being a bad influence. Reevaluates all of Christianity.

If you can relate to the negative characteristics in the right column, it's **not** too late. But you will probably have to exercise strong dependence on God's strength, using

Scriptural guidelines. Forcing yourself to reject any tendencies to lead an unscriptural life-style, along with rejecting the false excuses or reasonings that Satan will try to get you to accept. Also, you will probably have to fight the many temptations which Satan will design and throw at you to make you give up and run away from your marriage. And because the positive changes will not be instant, some of the hurts will continue and there will be a strong desire to escape. During this time of trial you should avoid all those people who would advise you to run from your commitment to marriage and seek divorce. It's easy for them to give you that kind of advice. They don't have to "pay the price" for your disobedience or experience your chastening because you failed to obey God.

If your husband has seen the need, and has purposed to change, he **will** change. And because he will need all the help he can get, you are a necessary part of that change. But, no matter how much determination he has, it will still require a lot of time as he seeks to become more Christ-like. Because you are already tired and worn down from the war that's been going on in your relationship, your husband's change will probably require much more time than you feel you are able to give. But no matter how much you want your unpleasant situation to change NOW, it probably won't and usually doesn't.

It is natural and scriptural for a wife to want her husband to become more Christ-like. But please remember, you cannot force your husband to change! Changing your husband is God's responsibility. Your job, as a wife/help meet, consists of being the helper that God wants you to be. Help your husband as he struggles with his quest for Christ-likeness and then you both can enjoy the resulting spiritual maturity. If you try to take over the responsibility of changing your husband it will have a very negative effect on your own relationship with God. This is why. Satan will try to distract your eyes from God by getting you to be **totally preoccupied** with your husband's need to improve. Then when your husband doesn't change in accordance with **your** plans and expectations, Satan will have the joy of defeating **you** with frustration, bitterness, and other emotions. So don't let Satan have his way!

> "So be subject to God - Stand firm against the devil: resist him and he will flee from you." (James 4:7 AMP, Bible)

TURNING TO GOD

I believe that women are more naturally inclined to turn to God for help than men. So, why not draw upon that greater tendency to include God in all that you do. You both will benefit. If your husband doesn't already think like that, try to find ways to help him develop this type of thought pattern: Before we do **anything** in life, we should try to reflect on it through God's eyes. The more we bring ourselves to reflect on the presence of God, the more we will feel his closeness and experience His comfort. However, while you are both in the middle of a stressful situation or trial don't be surprised if your husband resists your attempts to remind him of the need to include God. It's not uncommon for Christians who are in the middle of displaying bad attitudes to resist reminders about their responsibility to illustrate godliness. **It's natural** for any human being **to resist the things of God** and might even be less surprising to us when we see them resist if we learned to expect it. Even though we may learn to expect it, please let's not cultivate the type of negative mental attitude toward a husband or any other person that suggests, "Well, what else could I expect from you?" Instead, we should develop the type of mental attitude that says: "I'm not always eager to be obedient to God either (even though I know I should be) so why should I look down on someone else when they're struggling?" We need to build the type of mental attitude toward others that exemplifies patience and understanding.

TURNING TO GOD IN YOUR LIFE THROUGH SCRIPTURE

All men need to learn more about walking through their life with God. A husband is cheating himself is he hasn't discovered more about the nearness of God through oneness with his wife. A wife can be an example to her husband by letting him see her bring God into her everyday life's activities. That might mean letting him observe her reading her Bible. She shouldn't be hesitant. There's nothing wrong with having a hunger for God's Word. She shouldn't let the sincerity of her search for more knowledge of God become tainted, however. She shouldn't add to her motivation the idea of bringing conviction upon her husband. This means she should not be selecting times to read Scripture because she thinks it will be most noticeable— for more conviction. Also, she should not become "preachy" about what she's reading. Remember, because many men are already looking at women in a negative light, a husband might decide that his wife's real motive for being so outspoken about "what God says" is to be manipulative. Especially if he knows her relationship with God is not what it could or should be. A husband might even (out of conviction) interpret it as another demonstration of his wife and God against him.

If you have a question in your mind, some appropriate times for reading might be: early in the morning while others are rising, (if you are an early riser); during lunch breaks; before retiring, (while others are settling down); while the kids are doing their homework, and there's a need for quiet; or while your husband is reading the newspaper. Use your keen sensitivities to check out your true motives when it comes to your reading habits. Let your Bible reading be for **your** benefit. Your husband needs to see your **personal hunger** for God in action rather than seeing an attitude of, "Hey, why don't you get with the program and be spiritual, like me?" Even though you're longing for your husband to be the spiritual leader, you cannot force him to be the leader no matter how hard you try. You may be tempted to find ways of cornering him into something that will expose him to spirituality . . . your motives may be good . . . but don't let good motives be corrupted with improper methods.

There is a common reason why many Christian men aren't highly motivated to question their own adequacy as the spiritual leader in their home. They really believe they already are the best spiritual leader they need to be even if they aren't. It's not difficult for them to think they already are a spiritual leader because they are reflecting on the strength of their ability to dominate rather than on their spiritual strength to resist Satan and protect and lead their family. That's because many men mistakenly think that God wants them to **dominate** their wife, and that **that** is being the spiritual head.

I too am basically blind to my own inadequacy (or lack of natural ability) as a spiritual leader. I may be completely missing the boat while thinking I am doing great. I need to be awakened and encouraged to discover areas in which I can provide Christian leadership for Nancy and our children. Keeping in mind the idea of becoming more responsible as the spiritual leader, I've discovered that legitimate questions from them really draw me out. Especially when it comes to scriptural questions. I think most husbands can more easily learn to get involved with their family through questions. But I also think that most husbands can sense whether a question is being asked with a sincere desire to gain his thinking, or is an attempt to steer his thinking. So why not let your husband experience the joy of knowing that you sincerely think he is someone you can learn from? Everybody likes to feel needed.

Some suggested avenues of approach for awakening your husband's understanding about spiritual leadership include the following:

- Go to him with your scriptural questions about doctrine, philosophies, study methods, etc. Don't tell him at this time what everyone else said (unless he asks you). He may suspect that your real motive for asking him was just to get the opportunity to teach.

- Ask for his opinion on the material being taught in the Bible study you're attending or presenting. Did you remember to ask him how he feels about your involvement?

- Encourage him to share his thoughts on the Sunday sermon.

The time will come (if it has not already) when he will indeed be your spiritual leader. The aforementioned ideas should help condition you to think in terms of him providing you with direction, instruction, and even correction.

If your husband does not respond to these suggestions, do not assume that you are being rejected. It may be that he feels inadequate to answer your scriptural questions. Or it may not occur to him that discussions with you about scripture are an important part of being the spiritual leader. He may not **yet** realize that spiritual discussions are an essential part of building his relationship with God, you, and others.

I have traveled all over America, and have met tens of thousands of men, and know of few who have learned how to be a part of an on-going converstional relationship with their wife. It's not unusual to see men who, as a general practice, just plain ignore their wife's questions or conversation. Also it does not seem to me that women have been taught that it's useless to talk to a man if he's not listening. So they start talking and don't bother to make sure that they have their husband's attention first. This means many relationships are completely missing the boat. To rebuild your communication patterns, might I suggest making sure that you have his attention first. If you do get his attention and after you start talking he goes back to his preoccupation, stop talking and regain his attention. While he is learning to listen, you may have to find a way to **make your conversation as attractive and simple as possible.** That may be difficult since many wives who have husbands who don't enter into conversations at all, are also wives who ramble when they talk. Even though it might sound absurd, try writing down what you want to say and see how briefly you can express yourself before talking to your husband.

Now, let's suppose you were able to ask your question and he even listened. Don't expect an instant answer.

Be willing to wait a minute or two. If he doesn't answer you, you might ask him if he would like you to check back with him later. (Name a time: a half hour, hour, or maybe even tomorrow.) This will give him time to think about your question. Then be sure to check back with him. **Now** don't be surprised (as if you would be) when you discover that he has forgotten the whole thing. Be prepared to start over again. If you can, make yourself remember when you talk that his poor listening habits are due to his lack of training, and as a result he may lack the understanding that it's God's will that he value you. You have not caused his poor listening habits. Even if it could be verified or didn't need to be because you agree that you talk too much, that is no excuse for any husband to ever "turn off" his wife. Rather, he is required to discover why you have such an appetite for verbal communication, and then care for your need in this area. But all this evidence of conflict should emphasize the great need **in men** for change. Maybe you will realize by what we've presented here so far that it is going to require a great deal of determination to be a help meet. Obviously you will have to press on in the face of what seems like impossible odds. If you **practice** this procedure (patiently, striving to get his attention) then he may start listening better, but it will demand great patience!

TURNING TO GOD IN YOUR LIFE THROUGH PRAYER

A praying wife can intimidate a husband who is not praying. So, some wives are hesitant to let their husbands see or hear them praying. But praying pleases God and it's good for your husband to be aware that you honor God by having a prayerful relationship with God. Still, to avoid his misunderstanding your motives, you might need to consider the idea of praying during times that will seem "normal" to him.

Maybe the following suggestions would be helpful as you try to develop a spiritual togetherness with prayer:

• Ask him how he **feels** about prayer and let him know how you feel about it.

- Another form of intimacy can be experienced if you are able to share with him who and what you pray about.

- If you have children, let him know what your prayer concerns are for them.

- If your relationship is pretty good ask your husband if he has any personal prayer request that you could pray about. Then let him know later that you have been faithful to pray for him. (This request still might intimidate him if he's not used to being open about his prayer life.)

Being spiritually intimate with your husband might also include being honest about your own doubts and fears. If you struggle with doubts it won't defeat or destroy your husband to hear that. It will probably let him know that you're human too.

You might be surprised if you knew how many husbands are also intimidated by what they see as their wife's "unshakeable Christian independence and purity." On the other hand, if he hears that you are fearful or insecure, there's the chance that it may cause him to reach out to you, to give you "protection." Your prayers are not only important for your own spiritual life; you need to realize how important your supportive prayers can be to your husband, as he struggles to break free from the influences of ungodliness and strives to become more Christ-like.

While a husband is working towards becoming the man God wants him to be, some of his ways may continue to be offensive to your spirit. He may say with his mouth (even in prayers) that he desires to be more Christ-like, yet his conduct may say the opposite. When a wife asks her husband about this discrepancy her husband might think she is asking just to start an argument or fight. But don't forget ... even though you may have been the one to bring it up, it is God who wants him to recognize his unChrist-like ways. It is God who requires that a husband be a Christ-like spiritual leader. The fight is still between his ways and God's ways. If the struggles in your home are similar to what we've presented here, then your husband **needs** your prayer support!

While we're on the subject of prayer ... does it seem like your husband becomes angry, argumentative, or resistant when you ask him to pray? Have you ever wondered why? I've discovered two reasons why it seems so difficult for me to want to pray whether with or without my wife Nancy. And, as I shared my discovery, it was encouraging to find out how many other men felt like they could identify with me.

First, while growing up, if a man did not have a father that took time to be with him, nor had a father who was patient with him, nor one who knew how to minister to their relationship, that man will not have developed a pattern of **going to his father** for help.

Second, being conquer-oriented, when a man faces a problem his thought process will probably focus on, "How can I solve this?" That thinking reflects an attitude of "I must take care of the problems I face. I must be competent!" That mental characteristic of independence will tend to prevent a man from naturally reflecting on his need to ask his Heavenly Father for help or direction. That man has not developed the dependence of a heavenly focus.

On the other hand, by God's design, many women tend to be more dependent. God knows that dependence is a perfect characteristic for a helper. That is the role he has given to wives. A helper does not naturally seek a position of dominance. Rather, the true helper is one who will naturally be seeking acceptance or approval for "services rendered." Therefore, women are generally more inclined to ask for direction and seek to obtain approval from the one they are hoping to serve. That same characteristic of dependence in women is the reason why they seem to be more willing to call upon God, their spiritual father, for direction. We men need to learn to develop the capacity of turning humbly to our Heavenly Father to a much greater degree. I believe men could learn a great deal in this area from their wives.

The resistance in a man to his wife's promptings about praying further illustrates that many of the fights a man thinks he is having with his wife are in fact a battle taking place between that man and God. This particular problem about prayer reveals even more of the need in men for total surrender and obedience to God.

CHAPTER THREE

WHY DOES HE BLAME ME FOR EVERYTHING?

Before marriage, Phil spent hours talking with Jan. He spent every free moment with her. They took the time to walk and talk together and look at the butterflies and flowers. He bought little gifts that said to her, "You're special!" Whenever a decision needed to be made, they prayed about it; he always wanted to include her. She was never happier. Jan found in Phil the companion her heart longed for. They became man and wife. Within a few months things started changing; some drastically, some slowly. Phil started spending a lot of his free time with his buddies or watching T.V. The purse-strings became very tight and he acted as though she could not be trusted with money. He not only stopped including her in the decisions they made, he started controlling her decisions.

Jan questioned herself, "What have I done to alienate him?" She tried to approach him to discuss this but he was either too busy, too tired or he became hostile towards her. Not wanting things to get worse, she tried to let most of the offenses pass unchallenged. Jan was hoping she could outlast this negative "trend" and see him return to being the man she knew him to be while they were dating.

Months turned into a year and their relationship worsened. **But because Jan was patiently trying to be tolerant, Phil thought she had gotten her act together and everything was just fine.** Then Jan became pregnant . . . she assumed that this surely would change everything! And it did . . . but, it got worse instead of improving. But why shouldn't it get worse? If Phil thinks everything is fine (and he does), why should he look for ways to improve? Oh sure, he may think Jan is troublesome at times . . . but he's learned that given a little time she always seems to "get her act together." So naturally Phil has concluded that if he just sidesteps her bad moments they always seem to smooth over.

But all of this relationship turmoil is taking its toll on Jan. Her emotions are becoming more and more explosive. She finds it more and more difficult to conceal her frustration and disappointment. Jan is starting to hate Phil. More and more she finds herself emotionally out of control. Phil doesn't like what is going on and decides that **he** has had enough. He lays down the law! She reacts with greater hostility. Things are bad! He finally gives in to her **repeated requests** for getting help and goes with her for counsel.

As I try to help Phil see where their problems started, he reacts. He has a hard time accepting the responsibility for the condition of his marriage; the same marriage in which he agreed to be her leader. He cannot believe that he is primarily responsible for creating this mess. He claims he can't respond like Christ towards Jan **now** because she acts so negatively towards him.

This brings us to ... FACT #2 ... **Blaming his wife, even for his own faults, is normal for the average man.** In too many cases, it doesn't even occur to most men that they could actually be a major cause for the marriage going wrong. A man having a critical eye towards his wife (while allowing himself unbelievable freedom to do wrong), is not uncommon in too many marriages. I've seen thousands of men who can be caught right in the middle of being irresponsible and disobedient to God, and still not let a "little thing" like that distract them from focusing on their wife's problems? Those same men will talk for hours about all their wive's negatives while totally ignoring their own failures and irresponsibility towards what **God** requires of them. When I try to draw those husband's attention to their failure as the leader of their marriages (like I was doing with Phil) all they can talk about is how their wives need to get their acts together **first**; they each say, "**I'm** trying but let me tell you what she is doing, she's _____, and that's why I can't do what I'm supposed to do."

Although a husband may think in his mind that he is justified in doing so, he can never legitimately use his wife as an excuse for disobedience to God. It is wrong for him to claim that **any** of his un-Christ-like ways are not his responsibility because they are a result of his wife's offensive behavior. It is also wrong for a husband to excuse or justify his negative attitudes and actions by saying that his wife triggered them—they are merely reactions. No wife is **the cause** of her husband's un-Christ-likeness.

Sure, there are women who illustrate a definite need for

receiving specific spiritual care. Such women might have very negative personality characteristics which can be offensive to men and make it difficult for men to appreciate them. But it serves no good purpose to just point an accusing, condemning finger. Problems need to be positively and constructively approached.

Since it is not right for a woman to be a strong-willed, rebellious or unsubmissive wife, a wise husband will recognize that those characteristics reveal definite needs. He, then, should be compelled by the requirements of his role to learn what it takes to provide the care for her that will minister to her spirit and counter those undesirable characteristics. This same wife could just as easily be God's method for waking up or **confronting her husband** with his lack of leadership ability. Her character deficiencies could help him discover if he has the capacity to act (especially in the face of trials) in a Christ-like manner. Is he Christ-like towards her at all times? Christ would be! Or is he only able to respond in a loving manner if and when she's loving?

> *"If you love those who love you, what credit is that to you? Even sinners love those who love them. And if you do good to those who are good to you, what credit is that to you? Even sinners do that . . . But if you love and do good without expecting back . . . Then your reward will be great, and you will be sons of the Most High, because He is also kind to the ungrateful and wicked . . . " (Luke 6:32, 33, 35 N.I.V.)*

THE "BUCK" PASSING STOPS HERE!

The whole idea of getting married is to honor God's plan and sanctify a man and woman's union. As such, when a man and woman enter into marriage and speak their vows, **they have entered into a covenant with God.** Therefore, because of those vows, a man will stand before God and be held responsible for having met the requirements of his promises to God. God has ordained that the husband will be the spiritual leader. Whether he is aware of that fact or not, **he has** entered into that type of commitment **with** God.

Fulfillment of those vows will be required of **him** no matter what his wife does. And because God is sovereign and because a husband is charged with caring for his wife's spirit, a man **will** be answerable to God concerning her **spiritual** condition.

> *"When you make a vow to God, do not delay in fulfilling it. He has no pleasure in fools; fulfill your vow. It is better not to vow than to make a vow and not fulfill it." (Ecclesiastes 5:4, 5 N.I.V.)*

In becoming the spiritual leader of the home, a man is never excused from that obligation and responsibility before God. He cannot excuse his wrongs by trying to imply that he has been captivated by his wife's influence and is servile to her negative ways: He is not governed by his wife's lack of emotional self-control. Even though **she** may be out of control, there is no excuse which will make a husband's negative response acceptable to God. The position of leadership requires one to lead. The purpose of Christian spiritual leadership is to provide leadership towards Christ-likeness, at all times, with no exception!

Will a Christian husband ever fall short in his attempts to lead? Of course! But there is a difference between falling short and failure, and there is no excuse for a Christian settling for failure. To me, failure is discovering I'm wrong; realizing I need to change; recognizing what I should do to correct my wrong, **but refusing to follow through;** refusing to do what I see and understand is right. God knows that many of us have, in the past, settled for failure. Even so he still offers us forgiveness . . . **if there is repentance.** Repentance is admitting I'm wrong, turning my back on the wrong way and **pursuing right.**

However, we do not always accept God as our sovereign. Many Christians have made their own philosophies and rules to live by. Some of those philosophies allow husbands to use their wives as their scapegoats when those husbands respond to their wives in an un-Christ-like manner. How convenient and comfortable it has been, for men to develop philosophies which give husbands so much freedom. Philosophies approved and made acceptable by some in Christian leadership who should know better. How clever of that deceiving, destroying father of all lies to have tricked us men into accepting a philosophy that permits us, as the spiritual leader, to be irresponsible. Have we been deceived? You better believe it! All this misunderstanding and confusion is evidence of the serious need in Christian men to become so familiar with God's Word that they can know **what God really does require** of them as spiritual leaders! We men must not allow Satan to continue deceiving us and thereby cheating us of the joy that God has always intended we have in our marriages.

The value of the Bible is that it reveals God and His ways to us. There are many experiences recorded in the Scriptures which are designed to expose us to God's ways for proper responses to life's events. For example: in the book of Job we read that Satan could not have tested Job if God had not allowed it. Still, Job responded in a godly manner, even though his wife gave him emotionally-charged, improper advice. I believe that she dearly loved her husband and was emotionally hurting for him. I also believe that she was motivated to say what she said because she didn't want to see him suffer. I didn't say that what she said was right . . . I just believe she was misled even though she had good intentions. Job could have ridiculed her advice (as many sermons are prone to do). He could have used what she said to prove to himself that he should never depend on her for reliable input. Even though he was really hurting and under great stress (which many men use as their excuse), Job stood firm in his commitment to what he knew to be God's ways. Job acted responsibly before God, thereby also meeting the requirement to be his wife's spiritual leader (Job 1:6 thru 2:10). In spite of **all the confusion and negative influences going on around him,** Job provided his wife with responsible, God-centered leadership.

 The odds are high that there will be many hard-to-understand and disagreeable events that are going to put stress on marriages. As such if my relationship with God is out of tune, then naturally, the last person I'm likely to confront about taking the responsibility or blame, will be myself. My first thought probably will be, "**I'm not wrong!** I've done what's right." My tendency is to defend myself and to blame or accuse anyone or everyone else, **even God,** for my discomfort or for the problems I face. I may challenge God, and He might let me, but He is still God. I can voice my discontent and question Him all I want to, but He is never wrong. It is in my own best interest and the best interest of those for whom I am spiritually responsible, that I do not lose sight of the fact that God is sovereign.

So, even when I am facing an attack, a trial, or pressures of any kind from anywhere or anyone, I need to keep the Psalmist David's words in mind. As a man after God's own heart, he realized: *"Thou in thy faithfulness, O Lord, hast afflicted me." (Psalm 119:75)* David did not just see himself being attacked, he also saw God working behind the scenes. Even though David wasn't always obedient to God, he did seem to recognize that all of life's situations—positive or negative—happen for one or more of the following reasons:

1. **To strengthen us:**
     Through facing a trial instead of running from it; searching out God's ways for solutions; making application of them and thereby building our confidence in God's ways.

2. **To test us:**
     A. By letting us discover when we are adequate.
         1. We might be encouraged because in a negative situation we passed the test; we

responded in a Christ-like manner even though the situation was a surprise.
2. We responded right even when we weren't surprised. We knew a negative situation was taking place, and had plenty of time to let ourselves become bitter, but didn't.

B. By letting us discover when we are inadequate.
   1. We might have areas in our live revealed to us that have not yet been yielded to God because we were ignorant of the need.
   2. We might be reminded of areas in our life not yet yielded to God that He has already revealed to us but which we have forgotten, or have resisted surrendering.

3. **To chasten us:**
   We are experiencing the consequences of our knowingly or unknowingly violating God's ways.The chastening, thereby motivating us to discover more of God.

Understanding the above gives greater purpose to the events of life.

Jesus also knew that God was in control of life's events. He never set aside His responsibility to be the kind of Son who pleased His Father—by being obedient. Even when those around Him were not treating Him with the respect He deserved, Jesus never strayed from God's design. Jesus saw that suffering and trials were meant to be God's way of bringing him to complete maturity. (Hebrews 2:10)

In addition to marital conflicts, trials will come from many other avenues in life. Every man will have to face situations that have the potential of shattering him. As a wife, try not to panic over the problems and pressures of life that your husband will face. Remember, none of life's events are a surprise to God. If God is allowing those events, He has a purpose in them. For example, if you feel your husband is being attacked by someone, (justly or unjustly), do not react blindly—and in anger defend your husband. It is right to care that he is being attacked. But if you **close your eyes to everything else** and just focus on your hurting husband, you may lose control of your emotions and end up merely reacting to the attacker. That will benefit no one, and you will end up losing the ability to constructively be a help meet to your husband. Being emotionally out of control will make it difficult for you to provide your husband with the benefit of the feminine perspective. Also, God has built a special ability into women: As wives they will be personally affected by what is best for their husband. And yet, they are still able to provide their husbands with an "outsider's" perspective. That's an **excellent** benefit for a husband . . . **if** his wife will resist the tendency to become defensive **for** him. As a team you can experience even greater victorious growth through each trial. Please keep in mind that it is God's desire that your husband learn from **everything** happening in his life.

It is also **very** important for you to understand that God wants total commitment from a husband and too many Christian husbands are not totally committed to God. If that is the case with your husband and he is not searching for godliness, then God may have to shake him loose from his complacency. If nothing short of letting him go to "the pits" will cause him to surrender himself totally to God's will, then your husband may just be headed for "the pits" and you must be prepared to go down there with him. That may not seem fair, but when you are involved in the struggle of developing the relationship mentioned in Genesis 2:24 . . . **genuine oneness** . . . the possibility of going to the pits with your husband may be a part of the cost. That may sound dismal but all of life involves balance. To experience one side, there must be an opposite side: To experience hot you must have the contrast of cold; light instead of darkness; up instead of down; good instead of bad, etc. Therefore when you are spiritually one, you will also enjoy the opposite of going **down** with him, which means you will get to experience the **up**; "going along for the ride"; experiencing the joy and elation of your husband's being in tune with God.

There is another area we need to address while we are examining some of the contrasts between our thinking and God's ways. I'm referring to the problem which arises when a woman has been led to believe that a "good" Christian wife should not look to her husband to have any of her needs met, even those needs as a wife. Too often Christian wives are encouraged to believe that they should not even admit to their husbands that they have any problems. Many a wife has been taught (or has been led to believe) that she should not **ever** burden her husband with her problems or struggles because her husband often is already over-burdened. That might sound like a very considerate thing for a wife to do, but it could also lead to other serious problems. A husband might improperly conclude that since his wife apparently has no problems then he has been adequate in his role as her spiritual leader. His wife seems completely self-sufficient to him since she has not been open with him about her inner struggles as a Christian. He may also conclude that, "I'm not married to a normal human being!" Or he might think, "I couldn't even come close to being the spiritual giant she is. Since she doesn't seem to need one, why try to become her spiritual leader?" It's wrong for a husband to use his wife's desire to please him and not overburden him as an escape—neglecting his own responsibilities. But being wrong doesn't always mean that a husband will stop using his wife as his scapegoat! A wife's honest communication may help her husband eliminate the drawing of inappropriate conclusions due to her silence. Your good, but misguided intentions might be the very thing that is preventing you from having a better relationship. One which could develop through **open, honest** communication with your husband.

It's a fact that we are each at different stages of maturity and we need to experience the freedom of being honest about our level of spiritual maturity. Otherwise we will always be living under the threat that someone may discover that we really are not perfect after all. All of us fall short of the glory of God. The truth is that we are all involved in struggles with our natural-to-human-being characteristics. Even if we can fool the people around us, we cannot fool God. Nevertheless, in spite of the fact that we are imperfect, we are still loved by God and can be loved by others for what God is making of us. That's an important concept to grasp. I wish everyone would reject the tendency to think that we will only be acceptable if **people** never find out who or what we really are.

> "But God commended His love toward us, in that, while we were yet sinners, Christ died for us." (Romans 5:8 K.J.V.)

Please don't think that I'm saying that wives (or any other Christians) should be satisfied with falling short of God's standards. Nor am I saying that wives needn't concern themselves with responding to life in a Christ-like manner.

The question is, can any wife be **truly** free if she is unable to be honest and open, especially with her husband, about how life is affecting her? If you've been hurt and you won't allow yourself to cry because you feel that it makes you look like an immature Christian that's an awful place to be. If someone pinches you, what possible good is accomplished for that person or yourself if you act as though you didn't feel it? If someone hurts you, you may fear that it will ruin your reputation as a Christian woman in your husband's eyes if you speak of that hurt. However, by adopting this conclusion you may run the risk of preventing your husband from ever knowing that he needs to reach out to you in compassion. Especially if he never realizes he should reach out to you because you've always presented yourself to him as one who is **not** hurting. You may have **mistakenly determined** that a spiritually superior, mature, Christian woman handles her hurts by "suffering for Jesus" in silence.

If your motivation is concern for the reputation of God in the eyes of your husband, that's commendable, but let God take care of that. Even if God's reputation is shakey in the eyes of your husband, it won't be the first time God has had to face a skeptical husband. God still wants a wife to experience the kind of freedom that will let her honestly approach her husband, just as Christ's bride can approach him: *"Come to me all you who are weary and burdened and I will give you rest . . . for I am gentle and humble in heart, and you will find rest for your souls."* (Matt. 11:28, 29, N.I.V.)

Some suggestions for developing spiritual openness might include the following:

- As trials confront you or your husband ask him what he thinks God's purposes might be in those struggles. Let him see that your questions reflect a genuine desire to know his perspective.

- If you run across some Scripture that you think relates to a situation similar to what you two are facing, show it to him and ask him if he thinks it's applicable.

- Let him know when he does something noble and how it helped you see Christ-likeness in his life.

Even though the changes in his life may not yet be "earth-shaking", it will strengthen **you** and help **you** develop a more positive attitude toward your marriage if you will thank God and your husband for the efforts that he **has** put forth so far.

It will be **extremely** important for you if you can frequently **emphasize to yourself** that **your husband is trying.** As much as possible let your attention be drawn to those **little changes** or efforts that he **is** making. It will be emotionally defeating if you allow yourself the freedom to **concentrate** primarily on thoughts like, "He's still doing an awful lot of things wrong." Develop the habit of giving positive comments for even the small changes your husband is making, it will stabilize your own emotions tremendously. If you would like to experience the joy of your husband being more highly motivated (which will be just as important to you as it is to him), develop the habit of thankfulness by thanking God and your husband for those things that could be easily overlooked. For example, being thankful even for his **willingness** to change will enhance the relationship between you and your husband.

It is a huge struggle for a man to face up to his inadequacy as a husband, realizing that he doesn't understand his wife, nor how to meet her needs. So don't add to his struggles by letting yourself operate in either of these two common problem areas:

1. Don't cause your husband to feel as though you are measuring his success (as a husband or man) by comparing him **with other men.** For example: there was a popular T.V. program named, "Hart to Hart." The male star's name was Johnathan. Let's say that Johnathan does something that is definitely good for a relationship. A wife watching might say to her husband, "Now why can't you be like Johnathan?" That statement will probably have a very negative effect on your relationship. Your husband will naturally conclude that you are measuring him (**as a man**) with Johnathan. He probably will not realize that you were admiring Johnathan's attitudes. It would be better if you could say, "I bet that really made Jennifer feel good. I know when you do that for me, it really makes me feel loved and cared for." Those types of comments are **less** threatening. The very fact that you need to direct his attention to Johnathan's character, reveals a husband's inadequacy. An inadequacy that represents a genuine lack of understanding and a relationship **blindness** that makes a man sincerely unable to see that inadequacy. Your comments will cause him to get a glimpse of his shortcomings ... do yourself a favor: don't expect him to be joyful about seeing those shortcomings.

2. Don't cause him to think you are using him. Don't **belittle or ridicule his efforts to change** and become more Christ-like, while continuing to put pressure on his wallet through **extra** financial demands. You will make him feel as though nothing he does is enough. If you always demand more without

expressing appreciation, he may decide that nothing will ever satisfy your ambitions, so why try!

Both of the above problems illustrate the need for women to establish a pattern of measuring their husband **with Christ** and that which leads to Christ-likeness. If applicable, resist the tendancy to compare your husband with other men. Never measure a husband by his financial or social status. Nor should you measure a man's level of Christian maturity by the level of maturity in other Christians. Even though measuring him with Christ is a much higher standard, at least a man won't feel like he is competing with another "man" when he is compared with Christ. As a Christian, every man **must** come to the place where he appreciates and accepts for himself that he **is required by God** to strive for a greater degree of Christ-likeness in his everyday life.

> Oh, another very important thing: There is a **danger in reading romance novels!** They are not **needed** and no man can possibly match the performance of the **imaginary men** in those **stories.** Reading those stories will also increase your tendency to make negative comparisons and can very easily lead to adulterous thoughts.

If problems 1 and 2 are already affecting your marriage, it's very likely that you are operating on the basis of some negative conclusions. At some point in your life you probably have determined that it is impossible, and therefore useless, so why even try to achieve a meaningful relationship with a man. Many women, having their need to feel worthy as a woman unsatisfied, will conclude that "things" or status will **make them feel valued** or **will bring them happiness.** However, even if a wife does settle for "things," God does not intend that her husband try to sidestep his God-given responsibilities. There is no substitute for a caring husband/father; and caring involves much more than trying to satisfy relationships with the purchase of "things." "Things" or status will **never** fill the void left by a missing relationship.

There are **many** women who have **subconciously** developed an outlook on life which causes them to operate on the premise that their value is in what they own or who they know. Some wives compound this falacy by believing that their husbands are the source through which they will gain those "things" or status. This perspective cannot bring satisfaction to the need within a woman's spirit. Is this where you are? Can you determine if your attitudes concerning your value as a person are directly measured by what you own, or your status in life? If you have developed that outlook on life, you may need to re-evaluate all of your motives and goals.

Maybe those things you've determined are really important for you, aren't! Maybe things you've decided you **need** are, after all, only **desires.** Having desires is not necessarily wrong. But if they really are only desires and not needs, it would be helpful for you and your husband if you could reconsider and/or reschedule them if necessary. You may even need to learn now to make compromises. You could be looking at complete changes—completely different ideas or actions.

Based upon God's thinking, maybe your dreams and desires will need to be achieved in a completely different way than you may have previously visualized. You may have to learn more about being creative as you learn to re-evaluate and/or compromise. For example: if you always wanted a Collie dog and your husband doesn't like big dogs, why not agree on a miniature Collie? Another compromise might mean extending the time you have allowed for your goals to be fulfilled. **Realistically** you may have to wait another year, or more.

Talk over your desires with your husband and let him help you evaluate them. When applicable, be quick to let him know how pleased you are when you see a dream, or even part of a dream, being accomplished. That will let him know that his efforts are noticed and are affecting you positively and that will encourage him to keep up the good work.

> It's okay for you to share your dreams, desires and goals with your husband, especially if they are God-centered. Too often Christians think it is wrong for a wife to have her own dreams, ideas, and goals; and that a man is not the leader of his home if he's not the initiator of all the thinking, plans, ideas, etc. But Gen. 21:8-12 reveals that that's not true. (Chapter Four explains the value of writing out your thinking for conciseness and thoroughness).

PLANNING TOGETHER

Evaluate the following from God's perspective:

When it comes to plans, most men **plan** on getting married. You would think marriage would cause them to reflect on the idea that **two** people's lives are going to be affected. But most men seem to selfishly and independently decide upon what their life's course **will** be without considering anyone else. Often, it does not even occur to men to consult with their potential partner about the conclusions they have drawn about their future. Take that selfish mind-set, add it to the fact that many wives have also been developing their own dreams, and you now have a perfect setting for marriage disappointments and disharmony. **So many wives have been led to believe that it's improper for them to share their dreams with their husbands.** And it seldom occurs to many husbands (on their own) that they should ask about—for possibly including—their wives dreams. Unfortunately not many husbands have been trained to know that they should be interested in or concerned about their wives' viewpoint.

It frequently seems to be a foregone conclusion (and

many wives seem to operate on the same premise) that a wife's dreams and desires are unimportant, inferior, or of insignificant priority when compared to her husband's. Can you imagine the by-product of those unhealthy attitudes when you add to it this teaching: "An **adequate** Christian wife will totally surrender her mind, will, and emotions, along with her dreams, desires, and goals, as well as her physical being to her husband." But, I ask you, "can God honor a philosophy that takes all the dignity away from a being He has created? Should we devalue a being whom He valued so much that He sent His own Son to die for her?" Of course not! Still, that is the type of degrading philosophy many Christians have in their mind with reference to women, and the "Christian" marriage. I cannot believe that God wants any marriage to be reduced to just an opportunity for the expression of male superiority. If men's thinking is all that is necessary in a marriage, then that type of relationship doesn't require a uniquely different creation by God, it only requires a kind of male-thinking robot in a female body.

As a wife, you should be released from the bondage that makes you think that it is unspiritual to have dreams and desires of your own. I believe that God wants your marriage to enjoy the benefits derived from your learning how to communicate your heart with your husband.

The first step might be to review and consider re-evaluation of your dreams and goals. Did you develop them as a child? Do these dreams need to be updated so as to reflect an adult Christian's viewpoint? Some of your desires, though reasonable, might be impossible to actually achieve under your present circumstances. Be willing to accept that. Check yourself out and re-evaluate any **unrealistic, relationship-defeating goals.**

As the spiritual leader, it is the husband's job to help put all of the needs in the marriage relationship in their proper God-centered perspectives. In obedience to a God whom he sees as his sovereign, a husband should never de-value his wife nor her ideas and dreams. Valuing a wife doesn't mean that a husband must accept and implement everything his wife thinks. Valuing her means that he won't automatically disregard or dismiss her thinking as not being worthy of his consideration. He should never sidestep any of his responsibilities. He should never blame his wife for his own faults. He should always reflect on his obligation before God to handle all of these matters in a Christ-like manner.

CHAPTER FOUR

WHAT IS THE SOURCE OF MISTRUST IN MEN?

When my children **were younger** they did something very interesting that other families have told me their children did also. While being with other families, I've watched their children do this and in too many cases, what those children did went unnoticed. What they were doing was instinctively done and is designed to help them establish values in life. Let me explain: We (my family and I) would be watching television and something would take place during the program that was questionable or obviously immoral. Let's say it was something like the trail of a man and woman's clothing leading to a bedroom or a commercial suggestively revealing a person showering, etc. . . . my children, who were always sitting closer to the T.V. than I was, **would turn around and look at me.** They were checking me out. They wanted to see my attitude towards what was happening. They were measuring their conscience with my approval, rejection or passive response to what was happening. Their future attitudes, at that moment, were being formulated.

Scripture says that the training received as a child will affect a child's outlook later in life. (Proverbs 22:6). Most men receive their negative and disrespectful outlook towards women from other men in general and their father in particular. Each father imparts to his son that father's primary disposition towards women through his treatment of his wife . . . his son's mother. This allows us to present . . . FACT #3 . . . **Most men have an unGodly natural disposition towards women that is basically negative and suspicious.** This often causes some men to feel challenged by the most innocent questions or comments a woman might make. Many men think that the strongest, single motivation in women is to try to **take over** and **gain control** of men.

Frequently, society as a whole tends to misjudge the intentions of women when it is reflecting on male/female relationships. As a matter of fact, even women can often be heard agreeing with destructive attitudes toward women, berating themselves about their own worth.

> Because women are so concerned about being acceptable, they daily examine themselves (especially from a negative viewpoint) to discover where personal improvements are needed. This desire for approval makes women open and often even eager to accept as credible the negative viewpoints of men towards women ... valid or not!

Because men usually don't understand how women think and feel, they often suspect that women have devious motives behind their questions and comments. It really is a tragedy that so many men have such strong reservations about whether or not women can be trusted.

However, there are husbands who are receptive to learning how their "natural-to-men" ways are affecting their wives. While I'm giving those husbands advise it is not uncommon for their wives to make this comment: "Those are the very same things I have tried to tell him before. **Why does he believe you and not me?**" My response to them has been, "Attitudes ... naturally negative attitudes in men about women make them basically suspicious of women."

Men will more easily accept comments from me. Especially about observations I've made of their negative attitudes and actions in their marriages. While they often refuse to receive identical comments from their own wives. Why is this so?

The following are five basic reasons why:

1. There are no emotional conflicts between a husband and me. Conflicts between a husband and wife caused by past offenses (or prejudices) will tend to make a man close his ears to his wife, while being

receptive to me.

2. Because I approach him as a "fellow struggler" he feels no condemnation from me. Even though it may be justified, a man doesn't like his wife exposing his weaknesses.

3. As one man to another I will try to interpret the "language of a woman" for him by giving him word pictures. This makes it easier for him to see his marriage from his wife's eyes and helps to clarify for him what's taking place in their relationship.

4. I am not a threat to a husband's concept about who's "the boss." Because **a man** is teaching him he has no reason to think, "No **woman** is going to tell me what to do or think!" Because of the natural-to-men reasoning, most men think that they and their wives are involved in a power struggle. Since he thinks he is being challenged by his wife, the average man will put up a big fight to maintain his supremacy.

5. I always try to get a husband to focus on his responsibility to be Christ-like. (This is hard for a Christian to ignore if he says he really wants to be Christ-like.) Often, because a husband is so negative towards a wife, she will have difficulty getting past the first four prejudices. Many men are so suspicious or insecure about women that even a challenge to become more Christ-like is not legitimate to them if it's from their wives.

I have enjoyed helping many men overcome their suspicious attitudes towards women. However, even when men have been basically freed from their negative attitude towards women there will still be a tendency to fall back into the same trap. It's just not part of man's nature to consistently see tremendous value in his wife. Again, that's because we don't **naturally** see our wives from God's perspective. Then, too, there's the natural tendency to justify ourselves by rationalizing our wrongs, or shifting the blame back to our wives (or others). We don't even need to receive instruction to become such experts at shifting the blame; it's done without thinking. Isn't it interesting how all that craftiness is natural. It's additional evidence of how men, as human beings, have sins that come naturally and need to be overcome.

Men need to challenge themselves by making their first priority as a Christian that of **examining themselves** more closely. That singular type of focus will free a man from the distractions of trying to find someone to blame. A man could then put his **full** focus on eliminating his own negative attitudes and actions; negative attitudes which will affect him adversely and prevent him from illustrating Christ-likeness to his wife and others.

> Remember, a wife cannot force her husband, nor try to make it more convenient for him, to have a stronger commitment to Christ-likeness. That is a job for the Holy Spirit.

Contrary to many popular theories today, a wife is not the cause of her husband's un-Christ-like responses to her, nor will she be a deterrent to her husband if his quest for Christ-likeness is intensely genuine. It's possible that a wife may be a source of some difficulties for her husband. But those same difficulties can assist him in his becoming a leader, developing his Christ-like responses in the face of those difficulties, which will then illustrate to those he's leading how one has victories over difficulties. I'm sure God must be thinking, "I wish there were more men around who were willing to make the type of commitment that says, 'In spite of what my wife or anyone else may do, nothing is going to derail **my quest** for godliness.' " (See II Chronicles 16:9)

Let's suppose that a woman were to illustrate a high degree of godliness in her actions and responses to her husband. That's no guarantee that her husband will recognize what she's doing and respond in return with a Christ-like response. It would be easy for most men **not** to notice their wife's efforts because it's more natural for men to be self-conscious than God-conscious. For example, let's say it's your desire to enhance your marriage and you ask your husband, **"From your frame of reference am I doing or saying anything that makes you feel like I don't respect you?"** Don't be surprised if you get a response that shows a great deal of selfishness. Typically a man's line of reasoning could sound like this, "If you don't let **me** have **my** way or don't do what **I** say without question, you don't respect me as the boss." Because most men are not skilled in husband/wife relationships it's not likely that they would understand what a woman's motives are when a woman asks a question like that. Your husband will probably not recognize that even though you may not respect some of the things he is doing, you want to respect him as a person.

You need to realize that even though you really are showing consideration for him as a person, by asking that question, it does not mean he will know that you are being considerate, nor how to show you consideration in return. In most cases, expecting that kind of thoughtfulness in return will only cause you disappointment and hurt. However, please keep in mind that your husband's inconsiderate behavior is not a calculated thing. God-like consideration for a wife is basically not a **normal** part of most men's thinking, or Scripture wouldn't have to admonish men to love their wives as God does—as evidenced in Christ. (Ephesians 5:25)

Most men have not been taught to think about their wives in a thoughtful and considerate way. How many men do you know who had a "role-model" who showed them how to value and respect women? How many men have fathers who show a consistent Christ-like respect for their wives by talking to them gently and listening to them with patient respect? How many fathers show responsible cautiousness in all their dealings with their wives in order to avoid humiliating them or hurting their spirits? I am sure there are some thoughtful, considerate Christian men who understand how a woman thinks, but they seem to be few and far between! Isn't that a shame? As far as Christians are concerned, a beautifully radiant marriage should be the norm! Cases of emotional or physical mistreatment by **Christians** should be non-existant . . . but that's not the case!

Back to our point. Because men and women don't generally think alike, when a woman asks her husband a question she should give him enough time and information to enable him to get on the same wave-length. Especially when it's a question that is related to feelings. Men often slip through life without letting themselves experience their **own** feelings. Often when they do have an emotional experience they don't usually realize the value of examining nor expressing what those feelings are. If your husband needs time to think about feeling-type questions, show him that you're willing to wait while he tries to understand how to answer you.

I, myself, often need that kind of time to reflect on things. It's not unusual for me to need several conversations with my wife and much thoughtfulness about certain things before I feel like I understand what is going on. When I understand, I feel more comfortable. I feel less stupid when I think I am responding in an understanding, intelligent way.

Is communication a serious problem in your marriage? Here's **a helpful step** toward building the kind of relationship that doesn't always require drastic measures for communication to take place. When you have something important that you want to talk to your husband about, try making an appointment with him. (In writing, if necessary). Then talk to him about your particular concerns. During your appointment, **give him (in writing)** any thoughts, questions, propositions, etc., you want him to consider. Then be willing to give him time to think about them. This may seem to be an extreme measure, but I believe it will accomplish at least the following four things:

1. It will effectively communicate to him that you **value his time,** because you took the time to **gather your thoughts** together in a concise manner.

2. It will allow him to develop **more trust in your thinking.** After all, you took the time to **clearly express** your concerns in writing so that he could **follow and understand them more easily.**

3. You might **eliminate** much of the **lost time** that is **used in arguments.** Because you took the time to **think out** your wording, you will probably avoid most of the misunderstandings that cause spontaneous reactions or arguments in conversations.

4. You would be able to **convey** your **complete thoughts** or ideas **without** the **"side-tracking"** caused by words like "never", "always", etc. These words occur in most husband wife discussions and often lead to unnecessary arguing.

If your husband says that he resents your note writing, or as one husband put it, "If you can't say it to my face, then don't write it," let him know that the four points mentioned here are your reasons for writing out your thoughts. Remember the extreme lengths Esther went to in order to get the greatest results? (Esther 4:1-8:9) These four points are meant to serve as building blocks for better communications. Better communications will result in better relationships. **Meaningful relationships are the product of spirit to spirit (person-to-person) understanding.**

The following example demonstates a serious need for spirit to spirit understanding and better communication.

On our honeymoon, Nancy and I went to the Grand Canyon. Most of the areas where we stayed were lined with guard rails. These kept anyone from actually stepping up to the edge of the canyon for a closer examination. As we were leaving, I noticed a road that looked like it was not designed for tourists. It seemed as though it might lead to an area that would allow a person to get a closer look. I drove as close as I could without giving Nancy a heart

attack (about 1000 feet from the edge). I got out and walked up to the rim of the canyon where there was no guard
rail. I wanted a chance to look down into the huge gaping
jaws of that monsterous canyon. Nancy, however, wouldn't
even come within a couple hundred feet of the rim because
of fear. Looking down into the canyon I noticed the remains
of a car that had gone over the edge. Even offering the uncommon opportunity to personally see that sight was not
enough to entice Nancy to my side. Upon closer examination of the ledge I was standing on, I noticed that approx-
imately four feet below me was a platform about the size
of a large front porch. A very mischievous idea crossed my
mind. Looking back at Nancy I shouted to her, "Good-bye,"
and jumped down to the platform below me. I ducked my
head below the edge (I'm 6'2"), making sure that I disap-
peared from sight, all the while screaming as though I was
still falling. When I peeked up over the edge to look at
Nancy she was crying! I remember thinking to myself,
"What's the matter with her?" I couldn't figure out why
she was so disturbed. I could have seen her gasping a little, sure; but sobbing?! I remember trying not to get mad
at her because of what I thought, at that time, were very
unreasonable emotions. I can see **now** how insensitive I
was, although at that time I **really did not** understand. There
are millions of men in the world today who **do not naturally understand** their wives. Most men are not out to inten-
tionally attack their wives' emotions. It's just that they've
never received any training in these matters. I've counsel-
ed with hundreds of husbands who have acted towards
their wives just as insensitively as I did and it was just as
difficult for those men to see their errors as it was for me
to see mine.

In counseling with men and helping them to live with
their wives in a more understanding way (I Peter 3:7), I have
observed **eight** stages that most husbands seem to go
through.

First Stage:
There is an **unwillingness** in the average husband to

hear any negatives about himself or consider the need to **examine himself,** much less admit to any chance that he is inadequate as the spiritual leader. The first stage finds most men **unable to believe that they are causing any of the conflict!**

Second Stage:
There is a **willingness to examine himself** and **listen** to negatives. He is more willing to admit that there is a **need to learn more about spiritual leadership.** After many discussions about God's concepts concerning marriage, and helping them become aware, they see the contrast between what God requires of a husband and what they actually are . . . we've seen many husbands become willing to admit: **"I guess that I haven't been the Christ-like husband God wants me to be, and I see that I've been wrong in a lot of my words, actions and attitudes."**

Third Stage:
There is **a willingness to listen as his wife expresses** her perspectives about his offensiveness sometime later, **after** the offense has taken place.

Fourth Stage:
There is **a willingness to admit** that what she expressed **was true.** He will admit that he was offensive sometime later, **after** the offense took place.

Fifth Stage:
There is **a willingness to listen as his wife expresses** her perspectives about an offense **while** the offense is **being committed.**

Sixth Stage:
There is **a willingness to admit** to the offense **while in the middle** of the offense. This is a **very difficult** stage for both partners. It requires patience and endurance while the marriage weathers the emotional immaturity that has to be overcome before this response is possible.

Seventh Stage:
There is a willingness to let his wife tell him **as soon as she sees** a familiar offensive attitude **starting to develop** again.

Eighth Stage:
There is a willingness in the husband to accept as credible his wife's concerns **without becoming defensive.**

These stages reveal attitudes; attitudes that a husband will have to struggle with in more than just one situation. He may progress all the way through these stages in **one area** of his life, as an example, in the **area** of his willingness to spend quality time with his wife instead of devoting all of his time to his job. However when it comes to the **area** of being a loving, patient, encouraging father, he may have to go through all those stages all over again. Just because he goes through these stages once, it does not mean that he is "out of the woods." It takes going through many such incidents in may different areas of a man's life before he can more consistently respond to his wife in a manner that lets her know that he values and trusts her input. Like possibly several years.

CHAPTER FIVE

IS IT WOMEN'S EMOTIONS
THAT ARE HAYWIRE?

Are you questioning your sanity because you find yourself emotionally losing control over negative events in your marriage? Even though it seems like those negative events have been going on "forever" and you've discussed them— looking for solutions—a "million" times, do you feel like you're exaggerating their importance? Do you think you're defective because more and more you find yourself experiencing severe emotional distress? Well chances are, you're not defective, nor are you alone. Many other wives are suffering from the same kind of emotional stress. Maybe the following will help explain why you're feeling like such a mess!

Your husband may be aware that you are experiencing deep emotional hurts. You may know for a fact that you and others have explained to him the cause of your hurting; that it is a direct result of the negative relationship between the two of you. Nevertheless, you should not expect him to **comprehend** what is being said! The average man **cannot** see how he has had anything to do with **why** his wife is hurting, nor is he often able to have compassion for his wife. In most cases, neither will he be able to understand what it **feels** like to "emotionally hurt." If he really understood, his understanding would allow him to identify with his wife's hurts. The problem is, in their youth, many husbands were made to believe that emotions were for women only, or were dumb, or in any event were unmanly. This probably caused them to invalidate their emotions. Having rejected their own emotions as valuable, they will, as adults, be unable to see value in the emotions of their wives.

Most men are so **utterly** detached from their own feelings that they are unable to identify with the **emotions** of their wives. **They are genuinely unaware of the powerfully destructive effects their insensitive actions or attitudes can have on their wives spirit (inner-person).** At that point it becomes easy to mistakenly conclude that their wives' **emotional** problems, or the **emotional** problems in their relationship, are due to some kind of **defect** in their wives!

The following are some very common responses from

wives who **cannot accept** the previous statement:

"I cannot believe that he doesn't know exactly what he is doing to hurt me."

"I don't care if you do say my husband doesn't understand how he's hurting me, I don't believe it! And when you tell me that most men do the same things to their wives, I think you're just giving them more excuses. I also don't believe it when you say that most men don't understand how women feel and think. They know . . . they just don't care!"

"My husband cannot be that blind! No one is **that** blind! He has to know how he is hurting me and the children!"

The following is one of the most difficult facts for wives to accept:

FACT #4 . . . **In most cases, men do not have the slightest idea how they are emotionally affecting their wives.** The emotions women experience in husband/wife relationships are very foreign to most men.

I'm excited about the significant discovery made by one of the wives who participates with her husband in our discipleship workshop. This is what she related to me: "One time, I was trying to explain a situation to my husband in which he had really humiliated me, and he said, "You'll have to give me some specific details. I don't know what you're talking about.' I became upset because it appeared to me that he thought I was just trying to cause him more trouble. I tried to recall several incidents to help jog his memory, yet his response to me was still, 'I **really can't relate** to what you're saying.' Again, I felt he was trying to discredit me. I thought, 'I'll fix you, wise guy. The next time you humiliate me (which was becoming a common event in our marriage) I'll point it out to you while it's happening. Then let's see you deny it!'"

"When it happened the next time I said, 'See, that's what you do that I was trying to explain to you the other day!' I was shocked by his response. Even though my attitude wasn't too pleasant, he said, 'Oooooooh, that's what you meant? Okay, now I can relate to what you're talking about.' Because he was quick to accept his mistake it suddenly occurred to me that maybe he **really didn't know** what I had been talking about before. I thought ... maybe in the past he really was **not** trying to make me look stupid. He seemed to genuinely **not** have the understanding that would allow him to **quickly** identify with what I was saying. He just didn't understand how I felt and how some of the things he was doing affected me."

> Don't assume that because you did a terrific job of explaining something to your husband that his **acceptance** of what you said means that he **understands** what you meant. Also, if your husband does something that pleases you, don't assume that he **knows** what he did or that he **understands why** it pleased you.

She continued, "This breakthrough on my part helped me have a totally different outlook on our relationship. I now see that he was not trying to play word games with me. His willingness to consider what I was saying at this point showed me that he was sincerely trying to relate to me and understand what I was feeling. The awareness of this fact changed my resentment towards him into a new-found purpose in life, that of helping us become 'one'.

"If he needed help in seeing and understanding me, why shouldn't I be the one to help him? The removal of my resentment also allowed us to become a team in this new-found venture. My whole outlook on life and our marriage changed. I now have the joy of knowing that there is something of lasting value that **I** can do **for him.** I can really be what God intended, a help meet to my husband. I've never felt so full of purpose, so fulfilled, so much a part of him.''

Here's the significance of this wife's discovery. Even though she had heard me say many times in our workshop/ group meetings, that most men do not understand how they are affecting their wives, it didn't really get through to her. But now she understood it as a fact, and that knowledge brought a lot of healing to her wounded heart/spirit. That's not the first time nor the last time that I'll hear those words. Not too long ago, after I'd been work- ing with a couple for one and one-half years, the wife said to me, ''Because Joe has been developing understanding, the nature of his thinking is changing. His questions are less defensive and more inquisitive about me and how his ways affect me. The nature of his questions has revealed something to me that you have been saying for a long time but I refused to accept as true. He **really** didn't understand what was going on inside me!'' That changed his wife's will- ingness to be her husband's helper too.

Maybe your husband is not illustrating the kind of outstanding, spiritual leadership qualities that would for- tify your spiritual well-being. Maybe he is doing things that are embarrassing or disgusting to you. Even so, please, do not assume that he is doing these things to purposefully disgrace or offend you. Try to remember that in most cases, most of the things your husband does that **are** offensive are **not** specifically intended to offend or disgrace you. They usually are in no way meant to be a personal attack upon you. Unfortunately, most of those incidents are the by-products of characteristics that are natural to men. Characteristics which offend the spirit of a woman and also happen to be offensive to God. That's why men **must** become deeply concerned with their need to be trans- formed into living epistles.

> *''And do not be conformed to this world, but be transformed by the renewing of your mind, that you may prove what the will of God is, that which is good and acceptable and perfect.'' (Romans 12:2 N.A.S.)*

Sadly enough, those common negative male characteristics (whether expressed through words, actions or attitudes) all too often have the effect of making wives feel like they are indeed reject material. I am convinced that the chief motivation within a woman is the need for acceptance (from father, husband ... or an authority figure). Therefore rejection, or the fear of rejection, can become a very serious threat to a woman's self-worth and emotional stability. Even though a husband may not literally say to his wife, "I reject you", his lack of knowledge about those things which **will create feelings of acceptance within her** will have much the same effect as if those very words were actually being spoken to her.

Emotional insecurity within a wife can often cause her to subconsciously try to design "stop actions" which she believes will relieve these feelings of rejection. Naturally she will want to change her situation, so she's likely to search for anything that she thinks will help eliminate those feelings—the faster the better. And anyone who designs quick solutions while under the pressure of an emotionally-charged situation runs the risk of creating faulty solutions which could, in turn, produce more damage or increase that person's existing frustration. Especially if she's trying to change herself to gain her husband's approval.

Another thing for a wife to remember is this: If you went into your marriage with pre-existing insecurities and emotional problems, try not to cause your husband to feel that you are putting **the blame** on him for those feelings too. He should not have to carry **the blame** for any suffering he did not cause. If you do allow this to happen, it will tend to have the negative effect of causing him to discredit **everything** you say about **his** shortcomings. Your husband knows, for example, if you thought he was your knight in shining armor. He knows if you thought he arrived just in time to save you, and that you got married so you could get away from home because your parents made you feel rejected. He may also recall the events in your life that took place before you married him, and whether or not those events were emotionally or physically destructive to you.

He will not be willing to accept **the blame** for any part of your condition that was caused by previous events. And in all the emotional turmoil you're struggling with, please remember that even though your husband may not know how to make you feel acceptable, it does not mean that you are an unacceptable person. Don't let his flawed spiritual character convince you that you are unworthy as a human being. Sure, every person has flaws in his or her character that needs to be improved upon, but I believe that those problems which **center** around the husband/wife relationship can be traced directly to a husband's inability to see his wife from God's perspective. If he were familiar with and obedient to God's directives regarding his wife, he would be responding to her needs in a godly manner. This would assure her that even though there might be some personal shortcomings, she is acceptable as a person.

"*God commended His* **love** to us, in that, while we were **yet sinners,** Christ died for us." (Romans 5:8 KJV)

While it is my desire to provide wives with some untarnished insight into the character of men, I must caution wives who are searching for more effective ways to help their husbands become more Christ-like, quickly. It will be best while your husband is trying if you do not expect instant cure. **It will take a long time!** Even though your husband may receive the **most convincing evidence** and **reliable information,** it will still take **repeated** reminders and much ongoing effort to help him change.

There is a tendency in many wives who have been emotionally hurt by their husbands to feel the need to talk with others about their marital problems. They are looking for understanding and relief from those pressures which are caused by not being free to talk with their husband, and from having to hold back their feelings. If you find yourself in this dilemma and feel you must talk to someone about your situation—exercise extreme caution. It's difficult to find someone who cares and is willing to listen. It is even more difficult to find someone who is spiritually alert enough to provide real help. Therefore, please be warned, there are several serious, far-reaching, consequences which may result from not using wisdom in choosing whom you confide in. Here are only four:

1. **The damaged reputation of Christ.** If your husband is a Christian and you relate your problems to a non-Christian who knows you are Christians, you may be responsible for making them feel confirmed in their rejection of Christianity.

2. If you make the mistake of talking to someone who does not have a strong commitment to you and your marriage, **they will tell others,** who in turn will tell others, and on and on.

3. **You take the chance of receiving unscriptural advice** by talking to people who may be committed to you, but do not have a strong personal commitment to God and **His ways.** And, as is typical, finding yourself emotionally unstable at the time, you may be unable to properly evaluate their advice. This could **have an adverse effect on you for the rest of your life.**

4. Sometimes as others empathize with you in your emotional distress, they may **develop an intense hatred toward your husband.** This hatred might stay with them long after you have forgiven your husband. This may cause them to think you are foolish and they may try to influence you to renew your hatred. If they are unsuccessful they will become angry at you. (You see, some wives have let their husbands come back home but they never have forgiven them. So if you forgive your husband, especially if he's **genuinely** working at changing, your forgiveness will convict those other wives who didn't. So if they can get you to renew your hatred for your husband, they won't feel so guilty.)

Make sure you seek comfort from a person who is illustrating Christ-like character and who realizes that in serving you **they are answerable to God** in their ministry to you and your marriage.

An emotionally distressed wife is a very vulnerable woman. She is very susceptible to a "sympathetic" man. Keep in mind, adultery respects no one. Be careful, adultery is not just sexual activity; it is classified as adultery even while it is still in the heart. (Matt. 5:28)

When faced with a wife's emotional outbursts (pent-up emotions that finally surface) a husband might have one, all, or any combination of the following three responses.

1. A husband will usually experience anger,

2. feel accused, or

3. think that his authority is being threatened.

He usually will not ask himself, "What causes these emotions in my wife?" He will usually **just react** to them. Most husbands do not know how to look beyond their wive's emotions and look for a way to minister to the **needs** that are causing those emotional outbursts. You see, most husbands don't recognize that the emotional struggles wives face are signs that **reveal needs within their spirits.** A husband should let his wife's emotions be an indicator to him: Specific emotions reveal the specific need in her spirit and thereby make it possible for him to know specifically what type of ministry she needs.

Most husbands are baffled by, and do not know what to do about, their wive's emotions. For instance, let's say that one time during an emotional outburst you said to your husband, "When I'm emotional like this, it would really help me if you would **just hold me!**" You may then think, "Now that I've told him what to do, next time he'll do it." However, the very next time you get emotional he probably still will not remember to hold you. So you remind him that you've talked to him about this before and he excuses himself by saying, "Ooooooh, nooooo, this is different than the last time!" Still being in an emotional state you shout, "No, it's not! It's not one bit different!" (Now you have the ingredients for more fighting.) He will likely continue to fervently defend himself. Why? Because he **knows** that the **circumstances** causing you to be emotional **really are different** from the last time. He does not realize that even though the circumstances are different, his response . . . holding you . . . should still have been the same. You find it impossible to get him to switch his focus from **the circumstances** to **his response** to the circumstances. And now, since the argument has become so confused you begin to question your own sanity, right?—No . . . not right! There's nothing wrong with your sanity! What your husband doesn't realize is that you're talking about experiencing the same **emotional needs,** even though the circumstances are different.

Here's another aspect of meeting a wife's needs that most every man doesn't understand. Many times when a wife sees her husband feeling 'down' she will reach out to **touch him** because she wants to **comfort him.** She then begins to wonder, "Why doesn't he do the same for me when I'm down?" Why? Because your husband will probably not know that the behavior you are exhibiting towards him is meant to be an example that he can follow. It may never dawn on him that he should do the same for you. He doesn't understand that when you care for him you reach out and touch him to comfort him when he's hurting, and that you would like him to do the same for you.

Let's hope your marriage is still at the stage where you want your husband to comfort you by holding you. If your husband realizes he has let you down in this area of his responsibility (holding you to comfort you) and seeks to correct himself, if you push him away or stand there without responding, you will really confuse him. He will think, "If this is so important to her, why is she acting so resistant to it?" If you suspect his reasons are sexually motivated, then please, explain that to him. Then he will at least understand why you are reacting negatively to his gestures of care.

Here's another example, the scene is one of a husband who is driving home and has a minor car accident. When his wife hears of it she is concerned for him and wants to

be near him. When she arrives at the accident all she cares about is **how he is.** On the other hand, let's picture a wife who has had a minor accident. Her husband arrives on the scene and within a few seconds quickly observes the facts. If he looks at her and sees no signs of **serious** injuries, he might conclude, "Well, she's managing okay." So he goes on to the next question that's logical to him, "How's the car?" That seems cold blooded to a woman but very acceptable to most men. It is very **un**likely that the average man will totally ignore the car and care exclusively for his wife's emotional condition, waiting until she is emotionally stable even if she is **physically** undamaged. A wife could very easily conclude that her husband is a very uncaring person when he doesn't seriously consider the need to care for **any** of the **emotional damage** she may have suffered. Yet, in his own mind he is very caring . . . he checked her out and saw that she was physically okay, didn't he?

To further illustrate, here's another example: A husband lets his wife know that he has to go to the doctor. Hearing this she's apt to become alarmed. Her mind starts imagining all kinds of terrible possibilities, "What's wrong? How serious is it? Will he be okay?" She wants to know everything about it so she starts asking him a million questions. But on the other hand, when a wife says she has to go to the doctor and her husband cooly responds with virtually no questions, simply saying, "Okay," or "Oh yeah, when?", she will begin to feel like he is indifferent to her. However, from his perspective he's being reasonable and sensible. Not being as emotionally motivated his imagination is not as active, so he's not as inclined to respond in a manner that seems "panicky" to him. Although improper, he might be reflecting on a common male complaint about women and sickness . . . these women always seem to have some kind of "female problems" so what's new? Also, if he does realize that something might really be wrong, he may simply acknowledge that she's probably doing the right thing by going to someone who can take care of the problem. He may think, "It's in 'professional' hands so why should I step in?"

These common relationship misunderstandings happen because a man has not learned how to recognize his wife's emotions as signals indicating the needs within his wife's spirit/inner-person. Most men don't understand that caring for their wive's emotions is a very necessary and very important part of their roles as their wives spiritual leaders.

I watched a man make a major breakthrough in his relationship with his wife simply by reaching out and gently touching her when she was emotionally hurting. She was emotionally boiling and he put his hand on her hand out of curiousity. He was literally astonished at the affect it had on her. Right there before his eyes he watched the transformation in her emotions from up-tight to calm in a matter of seconds. Having ministered to his wife in this way and seeing the effect it had on her does not mean that he will always remember to do that again though. Each time his wife experiences emotional needs he will have to consciously think about what to do all over again until it becomes a part of his character.

Satan wants to use everything he can to defeat both you and your husband and frustrate your desires to illustrate Christ-likeness. He will not hesitate for a moment to use your desperate need for acceptance from your husband against you. Satan wants you to react in a destructive way to your husband's lack of understanding and he would delight in seeing you decide that your husband's offensive, natural-to-men ways are really meant to be personal attacks on you. Satan's objective is to thwart God's plan for you. If he can drive a wedge between you and God and cause you to end your marriage he will be delighted. Satan wants to tempt you into thinking that your commitment to your marriage is an exercise in futility. Satan wants you to end up with nothing but anger at your husband's insensitivity. Maybe the following illustration will help you resist Satan.

Let's pretend that you're a girl about thirteen or fourteen years old and you're attending school in an old fashioned country school where all the grades are in one room. You have a younger brother (seven years old) who is almost totally deaf. Today you have a substitute teacher who doesn't know any of the students. As she begins the class, rapping her desk with a ruler, she calls all of the students to order, "Okay class, let's all stop talking. Everyone . . . please turn around in your seats and face the front of the class." Your little brother has been facing backwards in his seat talking to his friend who is seated behind him. He doesn't see the teacher nor does he hear her. Most of the students (including you) are quiet. One more word and a quick rap with the ruler and all the students are quiet now, except your brother. There he is, still talking with his friend. You know how sometimes kids can get so preoccupied that they aren't aware of anything else going on around them. By now everyone is looking at your brother. The teacher angrily marches back to his seat, spins him around and says, "Young man, I asked you to stop talking!" He replies, "I'm sorry. I didn't hear you." Becoming impatient and angry at his words, she says, "Besides being disobedient, are you going to lie too? The rest of the class heard me!" Frightened, he replies, "No ma'am, the reason I didn't hear you is because I can't hear." He is able to communicate with her because he has been reading her lips. Not being aware of the facts, the teacher concludes that he is not only a disobedient, bad boy, but he is also a liar. She continues getting emotionally caught up in this situation and feels like she needs to assert her authority to establish control. She demands that he go to the cloakroom where she intends to punish him to gain respect.

Now, how are you, his sister, feeling about all of this? Do you want to cry out to protect him? Do you think she is unjust? Do you want the teacher to show more understanding and not be so unfair to this one you love? After all, he can't help it if he has a handicap, can he?

Could you try looking at your husband in the same light? If he is blind and deaf to what God's viewpoints are (especially when it comes to marriage relationships), couldn't you have compassion on his handicap? After all, he is missing some of the richest portions of life (the joy of an understanding, loving relationship with you) and he **doesn't even know it!** Let's help him!

CHAPTER SIX

LYING AWAKE NIGHTS?

Do you have a husband who does not participate in the "life" of your marriage or family? One who seems indifferent to you or other people? Although many wives complain that their husbands have "turned them off", it is usually **not** because of indifference. If those husbands seem to be oblivious to others and thereby offensive, it is not necessarily happening because of indifference. Rather it is usually due to ignorance about what makes a relationship work. That ignorance makes it easy for them to disbelieve that they are being offensive. A man can get into a conflict with his wife; walk away from it without its being resolved; come back fifteen minutes later and act as though nothing ever happened! How can men be so "forgetful?" Because they really **don't** know how serious it is. Nor do they know how important it is to **not** dismiss the conflict until resolved. They don't usually recognize that wounding offenses cause lasting scars.

Haven't you noticed, especially at bedtime, how quickly your husband can dismiss or seem to ignore a serious problem between the two of you? Acting as though everything is fine and surprised if you are not doing the same. He's not really ignoring the problem. If he seems to have just dropped the matter, it's very likely that he's decided one or both of the following: it's either not that serious, or he believes it **has been** resolved. This brings us to . . . FACT #5 . . . **Many men think they are very tolerant and should be commended for exercising so much patience in the face of their wive's continuously trying and disagreeable natures.** Don't go into shock now! Most men don't even recognize how much patience their wives are exhibiting by trying hard **not to give up** on their husbands and their offensiveness. I wonder how many wives think their husbands have secretly obtained a Master's degree in offensiveness and that they are struggling against a professional. Wives probably think husbands stay awake at night trying to figure out different methods of hurting them. Not true . . . men come by that negative characteristic, offensiveness, naturally; it's not cultivated.

On the other hand, wives **do** lay awake at night struggling with these things. Here's an example of what keeps them awake and why husbands don't seem to be bothered.

Have you ever tried to let your husband know that something he is doing makes you feel bad; and when you've finished sharing your heart you get the distinct feeling that no matter how important it is to you, you might as well have talked to a picture of him? It certainly doesn't seem to have done any good to have talked directly to him since his response was so indifferent. He seemed to dismiss your feelings as unimportant. Often when he does enter into a discussion with you, it's to let you know that your reasoning is way out of whack! It's perfectly clear to him (and other husbands are drawing the same kinds of conclusions), that the real problem is you. He thinks your mind is so out of whack that you are unable to reason soundly, so . . . why should he expect **you** to understand what went on or even why it happened. And so, having hurt you with his first offense, he adds to your hurt by denying that anything upsetting or worth discussing happened. It's clear to him that the real problem is **you** and **your argumentative attitude**; that's the real cause of all the problems. As a result, he rationalizes that you are actually hurting yourself.

Do you know that his motives really are not to excuse himself? He just doesn't see things the way you do. Let's suppose though that there was a misunderstanding on your part. Let's suppose too that you are confused about what actually happened or what you thought he did. That still does not change the fact that you were emotionally suffering, and that fact alone makes it improper for a husband to dismiss the issue.

Husbands who quickly become emotionally fatigued are another reason why wives are lying awake at night questioning whether their husbands even love them. Let me explain: After being hurt many times, a wife realizes that there is a **growing alienation** within her and it needs to be dealt with. She also realizes that to obtain the best results she needs to choose her timing in order to avoid further damage to their relationship. Let's say that one night she notices that her husband is in a good mood and relatively receptive, so she decides maybe this night is a good time for them to discuss some of those problems. Most of the problems are going to be somewhat centered around his failure to give correct spiritual leadership. She ventures into the conversation with a fairly simple problem for a starter. He responds relatively well so she trys another problem. As the conversation progresses he starts feeling a great deal of pressure from all of this serious conversation. Not understanding that relationships require a constant clearing of conflicts, he will not have been keeping problems settled, currently. Since there are so many unsettled problems for him to deal with he's likely to start thinking that her sole purpose is to attack him. Pretty soon he stops listening and starts defending. But, if he's not able to competently handle such an **emotionally demanding** situation, he will soon start to feel **emotionally drained.** His whole being will soon feel the need to stop this emotional **drainage.** He will feel the subconscious need to restore the loss of energy caused by this high demand upon his emotional system. A strong urge to sleep will come upon him. He will hardly be able to control the impulse to shut down and go to sleep. His wife will wonder, "How can you go to sleep at a time like this?" A wife is likely to see his "shut down" as further proof that he doesn't care. She reasons that if he did care he would want to resolve these problems. The amount of pressure you both will experience from these problem-confronting sessions will be directly related to how long your husband has ignored them; how long he's failed to address the problems; how long it's been since he's listened to constructive criticism and then resolved the problems.

While most wives are **struggling with the effects of distasteful events** taking place in their relationships, most men are **struggling with even wanting to face them.** Many men would rather forget them and want their wives to forget them too. Many men think it's unfair to have to live down past offenses (even five minutes past) and unfair that their wives would bring them up again. For example: if a husband's past performance in the marriage has caused

him to have a bad reputation (in his wife's eyes) then that
husband has the responsibility of discovering why his
character is suspect and work at becoming the kind of person she can respect.

Let's say a man has a wife with a suspicious nature. Let's
say her suspicious nature is not a result of her husband's
character flaws, but a product of her own past. Shouldn't
caring for even those needs also be considered a part of
a husband's Christ-like responsibility? It is necessary for
men to keep in mind that, as the spiritual leader, God requires that a husband minister to all his wife's needs—
without having a condemning attitude.

Here's another example of unconscious offensiveness:
Have you ever had the feeling when you were with friends
that your husband seemed to be doing everything he could
to make you look like an idiot? Did he keep trying to be
the life of the party by using you as his source of humor
and telling jokes about you that put you in an uncomfortable or embarrassing position? And when you tried to tell
him how he made you feel, he explained that you were being **too sensitive,** or that **you** were a bad sport. He alibis,
"After all, no harm was meant, it was just a time of having
fun!" So once again, he has made it seem as though you're
the one who is a mess, and you ended up being accused
of creating that problem too. His general attitude towards
you seems to be, "Will **she** ever get her act together?"

Please keep in mind that the way men and women think
and reason is totally different. It's very possible that if you
both were listening to the same story you would hear different points of interest and even come to different conclusions about the message of the story. However, because
you come to different conclusions does not mean that one
or the other of you has to be wrong.

Those differences of opinion especially between men and
women are often seen by men as a challenge: "Who is
right!?" And, naturally we men are inclined to believe we
are the ones who are right. The type of unconscious reasoning that often takes place within a man is: "I'm not wrong
and if you (a woman) think differently, then you (a woman)

must be the one who is wrong." This type of thinking is basically motivated by a spirit of competition within men towards women. That same competitive spirit hinders a man's freedom to develop an understanding of a woman's perspective.

It's an important part of God's goal for a Christian man that he become aware of his offensive ways and that he correct them. In our discipleship program for men, we have the joy of assisting husbands toward Christ-likeness by helping them to see more clearly what is causing conflicts and then helping them to find solutions.

Joe and Lori are a couple with whom we've enjoyed working. Once, while meeting with them, Lori shared how Joe made her feel stupid and worthless. She gave an illustration to emphasize her point. "We have this old can opener and it seemed like something was wrong with it because I was having a little trouble making it work right. Standing there impatiently, Joe crowded in and said, 'Here, let me do it. Even a five-year-old could work this!' He then continued to belittle me by talking to me as though I was a child, explaining that there is nothing wrong with the can opener—it was just my stupidity."

After hearing her report, I looked at Joe. He was looking down at the ground shaking his head back and forth in an expression of disagreement. After asking him what his thoughts were Joe exclaimed, "There **is** nothing wrong with **that** can opener!" I told him, "She's not talking about whether or not the can opener is working right!" With a look of surprised disbelief, he questioned, "She's not?" I explained, "She's talking about how you make her feel stupid. She just used the story about the can opener to prove her point." Joe responded with a puzzled, "Oooooh," that dropped off at the end. As he was reflecting on her illustration, it was causing him to re-evaluate that situation and his attitude toward her.

While Joe was giving that a lot of thought, Lori began wondering if he was doubting her. She then related another situation to further prove that it is common for him to treat her disrespectfully. "I have difficulty operating the lever that adjusts the car seat. And Joe makes a point of ridiculing me for it." Shaking his head again Joe began to defend himself, "There's nothing wrong with the lever on the car seat!" I re-emphasized for him, "She's not talking about whether or not the lever for the car seat works." Squinting his eyes, he quizzed, "She's not?" "No, she's just using it as an illustration to show how you've made her feel; how you're treating her. The lever on the car seat is only what she's using to prove her point." Still with some curious disbelief he said, "Are you sure?" "Absolutely!" I responded.

Lori felt certain that he was still trying to avoid facing the responsibility for his disrespectful ways. I assured her that his struggle was not with whether or not he would accept the responsibility for his errors, but that he was struggling with how to **see** and **understand** a totally different viewpoint. He was trying to relate to his wife by seeing what was happening **as she saw it.**

> If the average man sees his wife struggling with a problem, especially if he thinks she's brought it upon herself, he probably will not offer her assistance in a gentle, loving way by saying, "I know that sometimes situations like this can be difficult. If this problem is giving you trouble, I'd love to help you with it."

Several days later, Joe called to talk about another difficult situation that had taken place between him and Lori. After explaining what had taken place, he said, "Now tell me, is this another situation like the can opener and the car seat? I shouldn't get concerned about the circumstances, but instead I should try to understand what she's telling me about how I'm making her feel, right?" I was encouraged and happy to tell him, "You're absolutely right! I'm glad that you're able to see that! Keep up the good work!"

If you **expect** your husband to **clearly** understand something just because you clearly explained your thinking or feelings about it, you're probably going to be disappointed. Even when he's **listening intently** and saying things like, "Yes, I understand," or, "I hear what you're saying," or, "Okay, I agree," it still does not necessarily mean that he **actually does clearly understand you.** It could very easily take hours, days, or even months for him to think it over and comprehend it. You may have to explain it many times before what you're saying will actually "gel" in his mind. Then your thoughts and feelings will become more and more meaningful to him. Look at it like a puzzle. Before you can see what the subject of the puzzle is, you must slowly put it together piece by piece! So be persistent in sharing your heart, but allow him to have whatever time is necessary for trying to put together what you're saying, piece by piece.

Maybe you can relate to the following illustration which shows how things take time to "gel" in a man's mind: You're both facing a situation that requires a solution. You have an idea that is very good and you mention it to your husband, but he doesn't seem to accept it. You don't see any evidence that he appreciates or values your suggestion. Yet, you **know** it's a good idea and **it would help** him if he'd use it. Then at another time—hours, weeks, maybe even months later—you mention your idea again because you see that he still needs the help your suggestion could provide. But he still ignores your idea. You go through this process several times. Finally you give up on your suggestion and stop mentioning it since he acts like it's not important to him. Then one day your husband says to you, "Hey, let me tell you about this terrific idea I've got . . ." You stand there listening to him repeat back to you the very same idea you were trying to give him before, and you wonder how he can act like the idea originated with him!

Hopefully this story about a common event in many

homes will help confirm that it really does take awhile for some concepts to "gel" in a man's mind. He's not just trying to steal the credit for your idea.

As your husband realizes that there really are needs in your marriage and begins to work on building a better relationship with you, he may ask what you feel he can do to improve. Share your feelings with him. Then, even if you let him know of some specific things he can do, plan on at least one—if not all—of the following three things taking place while he learns to understand your suggestions.

> 1. He may **totally misunderstand,** and therefore **misapply,** what you have said. Thinking that he does understand, he may do something entirely different than that which you thought you had **agreed upon.** Don't get angry or upset. Remember to reflect on the fact that **he is trying** and that **he is making an effort** to show you that he cares for you and your feelings. Be sure to have a discussion with him again about this misunderstanding.

> 2. He might **totally forget** what you talked about. Please don't be frustrated. Remember, if he doesn't have an understanding of what relationships are, it will be very difficult for him to get a "handle" on what you're talking about. A "handle" which will allow him to "hang-on" to your suggestions.

> 3. He might **take a long time** to follow through. Try not to be impatient. Remember, he may need time to figure out how to implement what you've said. The whole idea of looking at life through your eyes could be a totally new and **mind-boggling** concept to him. Ask him about it.

It takes a considerable amount of time to develop a meaningful relationship. The idea of taking a long time is just as difficult for men to accept as it is for women, but it's difficult for different reasons. The difficulty for women is due to the emotional hurts they must endure while their husbands learn. The difficulty for men is due to their lack of understanding and frustration (which often results in anger) over what looks to them like an insurmountable task—one in which they expect to experience many failures.

I hope you've gained some insights here that will help you avoid some of those sleepless nights.

CHAPTER SEVEN

WHAT IS A MECHANICAL MAN?

After continuous unheeded reminders about the fence needing repair, Bart's bulldog finally got loose. Along with creating general chaos in the neighborhood, it attacked the next door neighbor's dog, almost killing it. Bart's irresponsibility had finally caught up with him ... multiplied. However, his wife was the one who had to listen to the children's crying and the neighbor's nastiness. She's the one who had to respond to the policeman's report, be embarrassed by the curious neighbors and pay the vet for repairs (on both dogs). When Bart arrived home, his wife was ready to vent her emotions. Her mind was full of negatives about Bart and she wanted to bring them to his attention. While she was delivering her appraisal of his character she said, "You never listen to me. This didn't have to happen. I've told you **a million times** that the dog was going to get out ..." She was so involved in her report she didn't notice that Bart's mind had side tracked. As though something very serious had occurred to him, Bart said, "Just a minute." He walked from the front room, down the hall to the den and disappeard. He was gone only a minute when he came out of the den and back down the hall with a calculator in his hand, apparently figuring something out. He reported, "That's impossible! We've only had that dog for three years. The way I figure it ... you would have had to tell me 913 plus times a day to have told me a million times. I wish you'd get your story straight! No wonder you've got so many problems!"

Problem solved ... Bart walked into the den, put the calculator back and turned on the TV asking, "Is dinner ready?"

If you ask, "How can a man do something like that and be so indifferent ... cold ... mechanical ... unfeeling, etc.?", then you need to recognize the following:

FACT #6 ... **It is almost unheard of for men to naturally identify with the emotions of others.** I am not suggesting that it is difficult for men to identify with the circumstances or situations of others, but that it is difficult for them to identify with the **emotions** of other people's experiences (especially women's emotions).

Men are motivated primarily **by challenges or the desire to conquer.** Emotions are not seen as a necessary part of this motivation. The central focus of meeting challenges or making conquests is **the need to possess, own, or control.** All of this is most effectively accomplished by **taking unemotional steps of action.** Therefore, most men will more naturally be able to function successfully and feel more comfortable when they are **mechanically** responding to life.

That's why men get impatient when they realize that a great deal of time is required to build their marriage relationship. Their tendency is to just find some **quick** steps to follow, do them, and then think everything will be okay. Their marriage problems will be fixed and then they can get on with life as usual. Their frustration is increased however when they discover that good realtionships are not accomplished with simple **5 or 10 step** formulas. It's also bewildering to most men when they discover that maintaining healthy marriage relationships will **always** require an ongoing effort. You might think most men would be comforted by the awareness of that fact and think, "Well, now that I understand that this is not going to go away, I guess I might as well accept it and prepare myself for the task at hand." Instead most men become **more** frustrated.

Contrary to the masculine, mechanical approach to life, women, are primarily motivated by the desire for good **relationships.** The central focus in relationships is **sharing life together.** That's most effectively accomplished by **entering into the experiences of others.** Therefore most women will more naturally be able to successfully function and feel more comfortable when they are **emotionally** responding to life.

Bart didn't relate to his wife's emotions. He was focusing on what she was **saying** and not on what she was **experiencing in her emotions.** He thought her facts and figures were mechanically faulty. This type of situation reveals the disparity between most men and women. It points out the lack of oneness between a man and his wife in the area of understanding. The inability to successfully bridge the understanding gap creates instant feelings of frustration and inadequacy in a man. And since he doesn't understand the reason for his feelings, he will not know what to do about them. His feelings of frustration frequently will lead to anger or withdrawal. A natural reaction of anger or withdrawal is to blame others.

Most men derive their sense of personal value from what they can do, or the challenges they can meet. They believe that the better their ability to mechanically perform is, the better they are as a person. Most women derive their sense of personal value from how acceptable they are as a person. The better their relationship with their husband is the better they feel about themselves.

This difference is brought sharply into focus when the events surrounding courtship and marriage are examined. At first, a certain guy's style is noticeably attractive to a girl. He interacts and responds to her in a very appealing way. She presumes that his actions are a result of his understanding of and **devotion to their relationship.** Then later, after marriage, she's very discouraged when all his attentive and romantic ways start disappearing. His actions now seem to be centering around his desire to enhance his own world, and seem to be almost strictly designed for his own personal gratification. Many women are deeply offended when they discover that their husband was basically motivated by the challenge to "make this woman mine." Instead of being motivated by deep feelings of devotion and a longing to make a commitment to his wife, he was mechanically-motivated! But don't forget, men are **instinctively** challenge-motivated; their actions will center around their need to possess, own or control. When honestly evaluated in light of relationships, most men's motives are not relational—they are possessional.

Men are **not** trying to be deceptive while courting, nor are they trying to trick women. It's all **instinctive.** It's so instinctive that it happens naturally. In a **typical courting situation,** seldom does a man set out to develop calculated plans which are designed to fool a woman. In fact, for many years I've observed this certain **instinctive attitude phenomenon** in **most** men. In order to help women understand what to expect or comprehend what has happened, I've boiled my observations down to this saying: Before marriage, a woman is treated as a person because a man wants to win her . . . but after marriage (in his mind) she becomes and he tends to treat her, as a possession. I realize that this is a very degrading attitude for men to have. But since it is an instinctive—not a conscious—part of their life, most men do not **consciously** reflect upon women that way. In fact, most men would **never agree** that those were acceptable attitudes for men to have. However, those same men might actually be acting towards their own wives as though that were their creed. That's why it's so important for a woman to measure a Christian man by his willingness to be Christlike **before** marriage. If she notices un-Christ-like ways, she ought to discuss them with him, being careful to observe whether or not his response to criticism is Christ-like.

Does all this seem like it would drive him away? Wouldn't it be better to find out before marriage if being challenged to become more Christ-like will drive him away? Christ is supposed to be every Christian's example. In obedience to God, Christ set aside the living of his life for himself to **unselfishly** do all that God required of him. He did that in order to restore us. Christ's unselfish example was also intended to show us how to have a meaningful relationship with God and with others.

It was stated earlier that challenges or unsolved problems are normally a high source of motivation for men. Unfortunately, a man cannot be challenged to solve a problem if he's not made to realize that he has a problem. That means most men will need to increase their sensitivity to and respect for emotions before they will even recognize that they are being overtaken by relationship problems. Too many husband and wife relationship problems (and even one persistent, unsolved problem is too many) are slipping right past men unnoticed, unrecognized and unidentified.

There's another major obstacle to overcome—pride. In too many cases, even if a husband does see conflicts in his marriage, it would be rare for him to **voluntarily, as a first line of rationale,** suggest that **he** could be **the reason** conflicts exist.

When characteristics which constitute quality relationships between husbands and wives are missing, it can cause a wife to feel emotionally out of balance. That can cause many wives to actually have a physical reaction. However, if they go to the doctor to find out what's wrong, the doctor can't find a physical cause. But of course, he can't. These wives are suffering from emotional mistreatment. It's normal (and I believe God-designed) for a wife to try to express her out-of-balance feelings to her husband. However, the average husband—basically a mechanical thinker—is often found trying to mechanically explain away his wife's emotions. Seeing the world from a mechanical perspective, his solutions for emotional distress (caused by the conflicts within the marriage) generally are going to sound something like this: "See a doctor"; "Take your estrogen"; "Get back on your vitamins"; "Stop letting the kids get to you, discipline them more severely"; "Stay away from those people who bug you"; "Stop volunteering"; "Change your methods", etc. And often his ideas or solutions sound so logical and he can be so forcefully confident, that you may find yourself agreeing with his reasons for your being "out-of-sorts", "up tight" or "stressed-out". Then you might find yourself concluding after all that the problem itself really is you—that you're just a mess! But an unfulfilling relationship will not be explained away with simple, thoughtless 'pat' answers. On-going relationship conflicts will definitely have a negative effect on a wife's emotions and that will cause problems in many other areas of her life. Emotional stress can manifest itself in many ways, such as being short-tempered, argumentative, impatient, overweight, unable to sleep, prone to crying, and susceptible to headaches, nervous tension, ulcers, muscle spasms, and many other things. Even though each problem area will appear to a husband to be separate and different, under these circumstances, the majority of those "emotionally related problems" find their roots in the unsatisfactory marriage relationship.

A word of caution may be necessary here. It's important for a wife (emotionally strung-out or not) to be very careful about deciding what steps should be taken to solve the problem—without her husband's input—and then taking her steps of action to her husband for him to follow. Here are four problems that could develop if a wife (especially in an emotionally stressful state), determines by herself what her husband should do to solve their problems:

1. If a husband is usually uninvolved in the decision making process (either because it doesn't occur to him to get involved, or he doesn't even know that involvement is a part of his husbandly responsibilities), then making decisions without him will make it easier for him to continue existing in the marriage as the "silent partner."

2. If a husband has negative feelings towards his wife and she gives him suggestions to follow and if her ideas turn out to be incorrect or incomplete, he will use this failure and add it to his list of negatives about her. This will prove to him that he has been right all along; in lacking confidence in her judgment.

3. If her steps don't work, it might make matters even worse if she has a husband who already is inclined to ridicule his wife. This will give him more ammunition to taunt her. He might delight in using his wife's "weird ideas" as his source of humor.

4. If your solution fails to bring the desired results, it probably will increase your own frustration and lack of confidence in yourself.

Still as men continue to fall short of what God requires of them you will also see women becoming so disheartened that they will search for their own solutions. Although it is not God's plan, it's not difficult to see why women could develop a focus which seeks to find happiness in the **"things"** they do or the **"things"** they own. So many women feel emotionally stymied and without hope, believing that their husbands will **never** come to the point of caring to meet their emotional needs. They question whether they will ever have an acceptable marriage relationship. Seeking relief from the powerful pressures of those negative emotional feelings, a wife may begin looking for contentment in other areas.

She may reason "If only I could go back to work I'd feel satisfied—like my life counted for something." Then later, after getting a job, her husband may hear her express dissatisfaction and say to himself, "All she does is complain about the work conditions, the boss, or fellow employees." Observing her unhappiness (in this "thing" which she said would make her happy), he probably will follow his normal, general tendency and discredit her thinking as unreliable.

Or she might say, "If we could go to Hawaii for a vacation, that would make me happy." Yet, when the trip is over, she still finds herself depressed. The vacation, this "thing" she had dreamed of for years and had determined would bring her happiness and would make her life worth living, turned out to be unfulfilling after all. And the misery of an undesirable relationship still exists.

Other expressions might be, "If I could redecorate the house . . . "If only we had a swimming pool . . . "If we could go out to dinner once a week . . ." So, here her husband is . . . mechanically performing again. After **doing** all those "things" **she said** would make her happy, he may conclude that he's **really** a great husband considering all he **did** for her. Now he is even less likely to search for ways to meet her emotional needs.

Seeing her discontent and dissatisfaction he's also apt to think: "If only **you** would get **your** act together and stop being so unreasonable and demanding, life would be much more pleasant." His conclusion only reveals the tendency in a man to function mainly in the mechanical realm and proves that he doesn't naturally have the ability to recognize the factors necessary for **entering into the experiences of others.**

More evidence of a man's tendency to misunderstand what women are saying: You're explaining to your husband that your son is having **a hard time adjusting to school.** You see it as an emotional problem. You support your belief with the following comments: "The teacher doesn't seem to be able to get his attention. He doesn't socialize with the other children. And he isn't doing his homework." You conclude your conversation with your husband by saying, "What do you think we ought to do about **it**?" Now you expect to enter into a discussion about your child's emotional problem. But your husband, who is on a mechanical track says, "what are we going to do about **it**?"   As far as you're concerned, obviously the word "it" refers to your son's poor adjustment in school. It's obvious to you because you easily identify with **your child** and the emotional factors involved. Your understanding of relationships allows you to exercise your concern about your son's difficulty adjusting to his situation. But your husband will find it difficult to identify the "it" because he is identifying with **the mechanics.** He thinks you asked him to solve several problems. From his frame of reference, he will have heard you bring up four "its." Even though you meant for him to hear just one "it," with three supportive, follow-up comments, all of which were meant to indicate the seriousness of the situation. But, your husband heard four points to be considered. His mind mechanically registered each item as a different topic and concluded that your son had four separate and distinct problems. When asking, what do you think we ought to do about "**it**", he's not sure which "it" you want him to address. Again, he's not trying to mess with your mind . . . it's just not as clear-cut to him as it is to you.

This illustration would be another opportunity for me to

point out the value of a wife **writing out** her concerns. It's a good idea, if for no other reason than getting one's thoughts organized before presenting them. If necessary (because of his past lack of self-control) mail your letter to his place of work. Then if it's a letter that deals with an uncomfortable or explosive subject, he will have time to cool off before he gets home. There probably will be events at work that will distract and hopefully soften his temper. However, the concerns expressed in your letter will still be sitting in the back of his mind. Although he may have been upset when he received it, one could hope that before he arrives at home the Holy Spirit will have had time to minister to him about how Christ would care for this problem. Your letter might even express that hope.

> This is only a suggestion. You know your husband better than I do ... let that awareness be your guide as to whether or not you should apply this method. One husband said he would rather get the letter at home so he wouldn't have his work problems compounded. Then she could disappear (go shopping or something) for a long time.

Since we're looking at the idea of men being motivated by challenges, maybe we could give some suggestions that might help you as you seek to motivate your husband—thereby turning your concerns into challenges because they are unsolved problems. A convenient form of challenging someone is through questions. Here are some common problems posed as challenging questions:

"Do you think you spend as much time with the children as **God** wants you to?"

"Would Jesus talk to _____ (name) _____ like you're talking to them?"

"Do you ever wonder if I think you love me the way Christ does?"

"Do you think that _____(name)_____ would think what you did to them was Christ-like?"

"Since I've gone to the doctor and he can't find anything wrong with me except my emotions, as our spiritual leader do you know how to minister to that need?"

Making a point through questions (even knowing before you ask the question what the answer is) is scriptural:

(II SAM 12:1-10) Nathan and David - "What would you do if . . .?"

(Gen. 3:11) God and Adam - "Did you eat . . .!?"

(Matt. 16:30) Jesus and Peter - "Who do men say that I am?"

Even if a man doesn't answer the question, it will get his attention and gnaw at him while it remains unanswered.

Women often try to motivate their husbands through "subtle" hints. Here's an example of how a woman might try to subtly influence her husband: After purchasing our book, <u>Discovering the Mind of a Woman</u> for their husbands, many women have tried the following methods to motivate their husbands to read it:

• Put it in a conspicuous place: on his pillow, in his briefcase, etc.

• Get a friend of his to recommend it to him, and then you become the helpful wife, as you happened to find it in the book store and thoughtfully bought it for him.

• Or (not so subtly), beg him, "Would you please read this?"

Unfortunately most of those women have said, ". . . He never did read it." Or, "He just fanned through the pages." It's a pretty commonly known fact that most men are not very interested in reading a book about how to be a better husband, or how to discover their wives' needs.

And isn't it strange how so many professing Christian husbands will settle for a miserable or uncomfortable marriage instead of actively seeking answers—**determined to find peace!!**—Following scriptures advise: "Strive to live in peace with everybody, and pursue that consecration and holiness without which no one will (ever) see the Lord. (Heb. 12:14 AMP Bible)

Moving on . . . there is probably only one way your husband is going to benefit from the contents of any book, and that's for him to read it. But you've already tried to get him to read books or seek counseling or go to seminars, and other ploys, haven't you? So if you want to be successful, he's got to feel challenged. The wives who followed the suggestion I'm about to give you, have all said their husbands read the book. In fact, one wife commented, "My husband said to me, '**Gimme** that book. I'll read it!' "

Here's a way to put your desire to have your husband read the book into a "challenge" form. Say to him, "I've heard that not many men are **man enough** to read this book **all the way through!" (It's important for you to use that precise or exact wording.)**

And from my viewpoint that statement has been true. I've not seen enough professing "Christian" men who are willing to take a strong enough stand to be **the man God wants them to be!** I think it's time for more Christian men to take seriously the **challenge** of a higher calling—Christ-likeness! Men need to stop feeling like they have to compete with their wives for dominance or superiority and stop working on how to get **their own way.** They need to exchange all their natural tendencies for the attributes of Christ. He was not a "mechanical man."

CHAPTER EIGHT

ARE YOU REALLY FREE TO BE YOU?

In 1980, Nancy and I had been married for 21 years. At this point I had been working on learning to live with her in an understanding way for nine years. One day in 1980, she said something to me that further opened my eyes, revealing a whole new concept about relationships between husbands and wives. All she said was, "for the first time in my life, **I feel free to be** 'the **me**" that I believe God intended me to be." I did a lot of thinking about that and it took me a while to realize the weightiness of what she had said. The discussion we had following her comment centered itself around what it was that made her feel imprisoned. We talked about her **need** to **know** that she was acceptable to me; we examined the lack of approval she received because she felt like the only thing I would approve of was a female form of Ken Nair (as a wife). We discussed the way I talked to her; the way I gave her "looks"; the gestures, sighs, groans and body-language, that all said to her, "you don't meet my requirements". She told me how I set standards for her that I didn't even live by myself and how those standards changed with my personal wishes at any given moment. These expressions are only a small part of what was revealed to me.

I was discovering the power a husband has over the spirit of his wife and what I had done to my wife's spirit. The nature of what I discovered could be summed up in two words: **extreme selfishness.** I had no idea how restrictive the attitudes in a husband could be upon the spirit of a wife. It never occurred to me that women could be so seriously affected by the attitudes of men; so much so that I believe a larger number of women, than might be suspected, are **not free** to be the person that God intended them to be in their marriage. The person they were intended to be is "locked up" behind the person they are trying to be in order that they do not experience the rejection of their insensitive husbands. And how tragic it is to think that all those women who are trying to gain their husband's recognition and acceptance—who long to be valued by their husbands—have husbands who don't even recognize what's happening (like my own testimony).

I don't think there is much consideration given to just exactly what extent the immature attitudes of men are actually causing women to experience "personality bondage". One of the chief causes for women feeling as though they are sub-standard is an unwholesome spirit of competition between men and women or husbands and wives. That spirit of competition causes men to seek superiority over women. The intensity of the spirit of competition varies from person to person for many different reasons. The **degree of hostility generated** within a man by this spirit of competition also varies and may or may not be openly expressed by men. Some forms of competition are **more recognizable** —yet even if it is offensive, may still be condoned. It is especially interesting to note that even in cases where Christians are involved, it is still seen as acceptable to be competitively offensive. The following are examples.

FRIENDLY COMPETITION?

The other day, while I was watching a young couple play checkers, the wife commented, "Can't we just play for fun? Why do you always have to play for blood?" Validating the attitude that most men live with, he justified his "kill or be killed" philosophy with, "What . . . and let you win?!"

VYING FOR SUPREMACY

Driving down the street in his car, a man is stopped by the red flag of a construction worker. A large dump-truck needs to maneuver into position for dumping a load of dirt. The man in the car notices that the truck is being driven by a woman. He is instinctively repulsed. This man might have thoughts like, "Another man out of work; Another woman trying to be a man; Because of this woman, another man is unable to take care of his family." But something much deeper is actually happening. Something **deep** down inside him is stirring. Although he may not understand nor have the right reasons or answers, something deep down within his spirit is reacting because he realizes that something is wrong. Many executives have this same inner reaction when they find themselves answerable to a woman as their authority, especially if those men feel that the woman is in a "man's" field. This is frequently a struggle when uniformed men find themselves confronted with a woman "superior".

COMPETITION WAS NEVER INTENDED

I know a man who had so much trouble with hostility towards women that he even struggled when a woman telephone operator asked him, "What number are you calling?" Something within him was triggered simply because she was a woman—she was overstepping her bounds by questioning a man.

There is a root problem here. It is a misunderstanding of God's purposes in creation. I wonder how many of these kinds of problems we would be facing if each man and woman had been taught to understand their own uniqueness and value as a person. People need to see themselves as the person God designed them to be. But, since most people do not generally see themselves from God's eyes, they will not realize nor appreciate His design for them. As a result they will not experience their true value because they will not have been fulfilling His purposes. This inability to understand God's design will be transferred from one generation to another. And that's why most people are struggling daily with the un-met need to feel valuable—striving to establish themselves as valuable. Often parents try to solve their own self-esteem problems by striking back through their children—trying to prove their own excellence by making their children excel—trying to "measure up" through their children.

I have to admit that it grieves me to think about those little girls who are being taught that in order to measure their worth in life, their parents must prove (or teach their daughters to prove) that, "they are as good as any boy!" It's sad to think of any little girl being taught that when she grows up she will need to "elbow her way in" to get her chunk of life—measuring her success by proving that she's as good as (or better than) any man.

CONFLICTS OVER COMPETITION

Our society reveals that many women have let a tainted

spirit of competition (in men towards women) draw women into competing with men. Women should not have to compete with men. They should not have to determine their success by how they compare to men. That's an atmosphere created by mankind, not God. The spirit of competition has at its core the need to defeat, even to reduce to disrespect. It is hard to picture competition as a word that would describe Christ-likeness.

> Because I know I'm in **very** deep water here — let's just stick with **husband and wife relationships as our focal point** while we discuss the value or lack of value **in competition.** (However, if you wish to experience richer relationships, may the Lord bless you as you search further to discover any or all of the negatives surrounding competition.)

The essence of this spirit of competition is hostility and it usually puts a barrier between men and women; thus causing them to measure their worth by trying to out-do one another. But women will never be as good as men. They're not supposed to be as good as men. Men will never be as good as women. Men aren't supposed to be as good as women. It doesn't seem as though it would be necessary to say this, but it is ... "Women are **not** men!" And, "Men are **not** women!" They aren't supposed to be. God created men and women with the same status and value, but they were not created totally equal. They were created unique, special and different—for different reasons.

This brings us to ... FACT #7 ... **Men do not seem to know that God created women to ENHANCE each man's life.** Furthermore, most men do not know how God intended that men be benefitted by women. Most men do not understand that the differences in the way women reflect upon life is God-ordained. The differences were never meant to be the basis for competition. We are supposed to benefit and compliment one another, not compete with each other. If it's true that on the whole men do not understand God's design in the creation of women, nor the value of that design, then those men are **not** likely to be thinking in terms of gratefulness. Those men will not know **how** they have been blessed by the Lord. Neither will those men have anything to share with their wives about how valuable their wives are to them because they are not aware of how or when they are being benefitted. **Good grief!** That's an awful place to be (both as a husband and as a wife) to **not** realize that, *"He who findeth a wife findeth a good thing and is* **blessed of the Lord."** *(Prov. 18:22 K.J.V.)*

Helping a husband learn how to understand relationships and learn how to value his wife can, depending on his frame of reference take a long time. Reflecting on that, some wives have asked, "So that I can plan . . . how much time should this job of being his helper take?" Even though I know that my answer is going to cause some frustration or anxiety, my answer is still, "For the rest of your life". Feeling over-whelmed, many wives repeat my answer with alarmed discouragement, "The **rest** of my life!?"

Maybe the shock comes because so many people have lost sight of what commitment in marriage really means: being **bonded** together—like an arm is bonded to the body. Sure, you can separate it but great damage is caused when you do so. Marriage has always required that a husband and wife be life partners. This means a wife will have to see herself as a life-time helper. **That has always been God's plan!** The type of marriage that God commands a man and woman build will require nothing short of each person fulfilling all of his or her role. That means **women must be allowed** to function biblicly, and in accordance with the vocational role God has given them: "Help meet". That name is meant to describe a vocational position which will be life-long and one which God decided was necessary in the framework of a marriage relationship. Romans 7:2 describes marriage as a commitment which binds a couple together until released by the death of one of the spouses.

After confrontation with all of this information, which reveals the total lack of understanding being demonstrated by most men, and then reflecting upon the emotional requirments of teaching their husbands about relationships, some women have complained, "But that's going to be like raising another child and I don't want to raise another child." I can understand how distressing it must be to live in a negative relationship and be told that part of the solution requires that you continue to suffer more stress and pain just so your **husband** might learn. However, some of that distress can be relieved by correcting an inaccurate focus. It really is **not** like raising another child, it's more like perfecting a partnership—or developing a terrific team. To keep from being emotionally defeated you really need to see the idea of a "long haul" from that positive viewpoint.

No man can possibly take care of all the needs of a family nor anticipate all the possible complications involved in life. But with a wife by his side **helping** him, he will (i.e., they will) be much more effective and successful at facing the circumstances of life.

> Of course, I realize that there would be more excitement for you in this life-long vocation if you knew that your husband were appreciating your efforts. However, even developing the skill of showing appreciation will take time. He will have to develop an **understanding** of what it is that **you are going through** before he can appreciate it.

It takes time for a man to stop examining his marriage primarily from his own viewpoint. He needs to realize that it is necessary for emotions to be involved in relationships and start accepting and honoring them. He needs to develop the capacity to understand those emotions. His wife's emotions need to become signals for him. They can indicate the condition of, or needs within his wife's spirit and signal him about the condition of their relationship. In the meantime, while your husband is learning to understand your emotions, you will probably have to be careful about the way you approach him with your concerns or requests, because he might just take them very literally.

I'm going to say something **very important** to you now. It is, **"Most men reflect on words by using only the literal meaning of the words. ESPECIALLY IN RELATIONSHIP SITUATIONS"**. To illustrate this, I'm going to use the third chapter of the book of John in the Bible. Here we see Jesus talking with a very intelligent, socially and politically prominent man. This man, Nicodemus, is inquiring of Jesus about a man's relationship with God. Jesus makes a statement, "Except a man be born again he cannot enter into the kingdom of God." If he were using today's language, Nicodemus might have said, "That's pretty stupid. How can a full grown man get back into his mother's womb?" Jesus had to explain to Nicodemus that he would have to start **a new type** of life. One in which he would have to have **a fresh start** in order to grow into **a new way** of thinking, with new words and actions. Without going into more about that chapter of John, can you see how this part shows that men mostly function on the literal meaning of words?

Let me give you another illustrations:

One wife, having had enough, (due to an on-going stressful relationship) tried to impress her husband with the intensity of her frustration by saying, "I think the only solution to our problems is for me to divorce you!" The next day she saw him sitting at the kitchen table writing. When she asked him what he was doing he said, "Trying to figure out how to split up our possessions." He wanted to make sure she only got what he thought was her share. She was flabbergasted. Caught off guard by his statement she questioned why he was doing that. "I thought you said you were going to get a divorce," he said defensively. "NO!" she retorted, "You don't understand anything I say, do you!?" But **he** thought he understood her perfectly. And while he did understand her words, that's all he understood.

Part of the tragedy in these conflicts is that many a man is absolutely convinced that he is **not**, in any way, a part of the confusion or problem. (See John 3:19-21, Prov. 14:12, 16:2, 21:2). Thinking and reasoning **as a man** will prevent him from seeing both sides. But he **will** see one side very clearly: his own. It will seem clear to him that **his wife** is the major source of their marriage problems. His reasoning will also tell him that he's being irresponsible if he does not make it his duty to straighten her out. Because the normal man is so blind and prejudiced, he usually won't recognize when or if he is a major contributor to the problem. Not comprehending the causes of marriage problems is trouble enough, but when a man doesn't know how to solve those problems either, you've got death waiting in the wings. Add to all that gloom a wife who is feeling all that emotional turmoil—and you can see why the divorce statistics in America are skyrocketing.

> I personally believe that the primary reason that problems exist in most marriages, is because husbands **either** are the source of the problems and/or, they do not know how to solve the problems.

Even though most men will admit that they do not understand their wives' thinking or emotions or how to effectively respond to their wives, they will not readily admit that that inadequacy has any relationship to their marital problems. Therefore, when it comes to conflicts or differences in the marriage, the average husband is convinced that **he** is not the one who needs to get his act together! Pride is very defensive!

CONFLICTS OVER CONVICTIONS

It's inspiring to see men with strong convictions, who are willing to stand by those convictions with determination in spite of the odds. However, the first consideration in developing a Christian conviction should be: is this conviction based on **my** ways or **God's** ways. Since the Scriptures reveal that all men are not naturally inclined towards God, I think it best that all men examine themselves carefully in the light of Scripture to see if they are actually incorporating God's ways. Having developed a conviction about God's ways, a man needs to next concern himself with, also implementing it in God's way. I believe a man will experience more confidence about his convictions being in tune with God (and about ministering in God's behalf), if he will reflect on them from his wife's **tenderheartedness.** Many wives can also help their husbands determine the most effective way of implementing those convictions **without damaging relationships** along the way. But, even seeking his wife's perspective will require that a husband have a strong conviction. One in which he has a commitment to honor his wife as a God-created person—believing that the expression of her perspective has a legitimate function within the marriage. I cannot see how a man can become a more understanding person if he does not learn how to highly value is wife's feelings, emotions and opinions. Even the "world" recognizes that women seem to have some kind of extra-sensory perception—they call it feminine intuition! I look forward to a time when more of those men who claim to be Christians are willing to learn more about the God designed value of women, recognizing a woman's ability to help a man become **more** aware of additional (maybe even advantageous) perspectives. It doesn't take too much research to discover that the celebrated position we have just recognized for women is not a commonly accepted perspective. It's not typical for husbands to **first** receive what their wives have to say in a positive light rather than in a negative light. Even those men who had been taught by Jesus struggled with this problem. See Luke 24:8-11 and Acts 12:14-16. When those women (in those sections of Scripture) gave valid information to the disciples, the disciples totally discredited them. The disciples thought that what these women were saying was nonsense. In too many cases, when a wife expresses her opinions, cautions or concerns, she's likely to experience rejection or resentment from her husband. Not necessarily just because he didn't agree with her, but in too many cases simply because **she's a woman** who is expressing herself. Even so ladies, please keep this in mind: Men's negative attitudes toward you are not necessarily designed with the sole motive of being personal attacks. If you can, try to let these thoughts become your natural reflections: Men are generally not operating with a high degree of relationship awareness. Not being familiar with the requirements of relationships will make many men feel uncomfortable and therefore inadequate. Most men will find themselves reacting to their wives as a result of these unfamiliar feelings. These differences between husbands and wives may be seen by many men as: someone is right and someone is wrong—it then becomes a contest—which in turn, makes many men reason that their wives are attempting to compete with or challenge them. This thinking causes them to conclude that they had better **defend themselves; they must resist** or go against **this threat to their roles as leaders.**

You might say, "Well, he sure seems to be able to build a good relationship with his customers/boss/employees, etc.! So why is it so difficult for him to have a good relationship with me?" It would be important to keep this in mind: Because a woman reflects on life "relationship-wise," she will usually think her husband is reflecting that way also. But that is not usually so. Although your husband might seem to be able to build and be concerned about relationships in other situations (such as his job), his concern is not **centered** around the desire to have a relationship for the relationship's sake, but rather around the motivation of being mechanically **responsible.** He realizes the need for caution in order that he **not lose** his job—keeping that which allows him to meet **his goal** of **bettering himself.**

CONFLICTS OVER MATERIALISM

The true motivation of many men is proven when their families (where the husband/father is labeled a work-aholic) express that they wish their husband/father would spend more time with them and those men say they can't. Many a husband's excuses for working so hard and so long are to have bigger, better houses; newer, nicer cars; fancier furniture, etc., **for their family.** However, if the family insists that they would settle for less materially and asks him to re-evaluate **his** goals, he might still insist that **his goals** are for the good of his family. It's not unusual for a man to fail to recognize that those goals he says are for the family are in fact **more important to him.** Naturally, then, he's baffled, frustrated or angry when the family insists, "If you really want what's **best** for **us** then spend more time with us!" You see, he equates best with the **mechanics** of best: more; bigger; better; prettier; fancier; faster. He probably doesn't realize that a wife equate best with the **emotions** of best: Times together; memory building; intimate talks and walks; the family laughing together; being best friends with family members; caring for one another; poetry; flowers; understanding and valuing one another.

CONFLICTS OVER HOME RELATED PROJECTS

One other point . . . if you have a project that your husband has agreed to do for you, you might take away his joy (in doing it for you) if you put him on a "time clock" for completing it. It may take longer to finish, or cost more to accomplish, than either of you suspected. If you make him your "slave," he will not like that position, and if he does submit to that position, you will find that you do not like him there either. These cautions do not apply if you are thinking about a project he started and did not finish because he lost interest. A loss of interest is demonstrated by the fact that the project has been untouched or incomplete for six months or even a year or two. That's just plain irresponsibility and your concern is justified; he does need to learn how to be more reliable.

One thing that helped me to become more reliable (and

also helped my wife to see how much really was being accomplished) was to have Nancy make a list of projects to be done and then post it on the refrigerator, crossing off each project only after it was completed. Here's what my list looked like:

DATE POSTED	PROJECT	STARTED	DATE	COMPLETED	DATE
10-3	Fix lawn mower wheel	☒	10-10	☒	10-10
10-6	Fix front door screen	☒	10-10	☐	
10-10	Wash windows	☒	10-14	☐	
10-10	Fix dripping faucet	☒	10-14	☒	10-14

This list became a challenge to me. The projects listed kept the goals before me; something for me to conquer. Maybe a list like this will help your husband too. Maybe it will motivate him and make him uncomfortable as he sees this constant reminder of unfinished jobs. It could represent challenges that remain unconquered and will hopefully inspire him to complete them. Maybe you could start with a list of only those jobs he has actually started. That list might motivate him upon seeing things he could have finished but didn't.

Sometimes the reason I leave a job unfinished is because I get so busy with other things that I forget that it's not yet finished. But Nancy may not know why I've not completed the project. A list really helps me and relieves her (to a degree) because she doesn't feel like she has to be the "heavy", by reminding me all the time. And since she's **not** a nag, she won't have to feel like she is. Most wives don't like to be the ones who are constantly having to remind their husbands. Even though some men might think wives enjoy it because it seems to those husbands as though it gives their wives a chance to aggravate them.

CONFLICTS OVER THE LACK OF FREEDOM TO BE HONEST

Many women are struggling with confused feelings, not sure of what to do or how to act. I think a large portion of this confusion is due to the fact that men (most of whom admit to ignorance about women) are making the rules for women to live by. And too many of those rules do not reflect God's best for women. For example: Have you been taught to believe that honestly acknowledging negative charcteristics about your husband is being disloyal? That it's disloyal to give a bad report about your husband—to your husband? Or if you let your husband know that he is failing, as a Christian, to illustrate Christ, that that's the same as being unsubmissive and shows bad attitudes? Have you been taught to believe that acknowledging negatives in your husbands character actually reveals bad attitudes in you—you have a lack of trust in God—otherwise you would wait for God to show him? Or that you are selfish because you are unwilling to endure trials? Have you heard that if you recognize all these problems in your relationship, it actually reveals unsubmissive attitudes in yourself? And so how dare you (with all these failings in your own life) go to your husband about **any** of **his** offensive ways, etc.?! Excuse me if I seem harsh . . . but BALONY! You don't solve any problem by denying that it is in fact a problem; especially if the method you have chosen for ignoring the problem is self-condemnation.

Do we not discipline our children when **they're** wrong even though **we** make mistakes too? Do we not testify about the regenerating salvation of Jesus Christ even though there are times when we do not act as though we are saved? And if you think that the only solution to your husband's relationship problems (with God and with you) is to just patiently wait for your husband to realize them, you may be in for a L-O-N-G wait. If your husband is **blind** to the fact that there is a problem in your relationship, **he may never discover it on his own!**

If a wife has settled for silence as the solution to her problems, I do not believe she is being responsible to her God-given role of helping her husband see the truth. If she says (or acts like) everything in their relationship is fine when she really knows it is not, then she is keeping the truth from her husband. Do we make a woman who is harboring dishonesty, measure herself as a good Christian wife when she keeps silent? Actually we are teaching her to give refuge to a lie. That approach will help to cement problems in a marriage. Because, if a husband is blind to husband/wife relationships, and a wife does not help him see, she is not fulfilling her God-given **responsibility as a helper.** Her husband, as a result, is likely to continue in his blindness. However, just because it's a wife's God-given responsibility, don't expect a husband to rejoice when he hears about his shortcomings. As Scripture reports, few men want to know about their bad points:

> *"This is the verdict: Light has come into the world, but men loved darkness instead of light because their deeds were evil. Everyone who does evil hates the light, and will not come into the light for fear that his deeds will be exposed. But whoever lives by the truth comes into the light, so that it may be seen plainly that what he has done has been done through God." (John 3:19-21 N.I.V.)*

CONFLICTS OVER DEFINITIONS

In Genesis 2:18, God said "I will make him a help meet **for** him." Because a wife is a **helper**—a completor, not a competitor—and men have not looked upon wives as an essential source of help, **what guidelines should a husband use** as he tries to define for himself, what the God-given duties are of this one who was designed to **help him**—complete him?

Here we are again faced with the problem expressed in the preface of this book—men's ownership mentality—which can be overcome by defining the word "for". Since there are so many different uses the word "for" can have, let me illustrate two definitions which will both reveal and solve the problem. The first usage, which I believe is the cause of the problem and yet is the most commonly held is, **For:** to be owned by—to serve the purposes of the owner, to **have** power over. The second usage, which I do not believe is common, nor generally considered, but would solve the problem because I believe it is closest to God's intent is, **For:** to allow something to be completed by—to be an addition to—having a positive affect upon.

Maybe this illustration will be helpful. Suppose you have

a child who requires medication (that has been sweetened for his comfort) even though he doesn't feel sick—and he is reflecting upon his medicine: He says, "Oh boy, is this sweet stuff for me to consume?"—oblivious to his need. Seldom will a child think, "Even though I don't feel like I am needy, I know that I am. And I'm so grateful that you would go to all the trouble of making something that will make me better, sweet too." See the difference in the focus? The first is selfish: sweet—**for me.** The second is grateful: I am in need. Thanks for providing me help! Both perspectives are based upon attitudes.

But selfish attitudes have been the rule as men have attempted to define God's design for this helper/completor. Generally, men have decided that the following are the reasons for woman's creation:

A cook for a man!
A man doesn't **need** to get married (gain a wife) to have meals prepared for him.

A housekeeper for a man!
A man doesn't **need** to get married (gain a wife) to get his house kept!

A sex partner for a man!
Especially in today's society, a man doesn't **need** to get married (gain a wife) to merely have a release for his sensual nature! In fact, if this is his basic motivation for marriage, it would be better for both if he did not try to camoflage his lust under the disguise of a commitment to marriage. Sensuality is a poor and selfish motivation for marriage. Also, discovering that satisfying his sensual nature was his central consideration for marriage, a wife could easily feel as though she were emotionally and physically violated.

The first two "typical reasons" just mentioned for marriage can be satisfied without having to take a wife. All three reasons show a far less-than-godly focus in a man. They do not reflect upon what God had in mind when **He** designed the help meet—completor.

The guideline, I believe a husband should keep in mind

as he defines the duties of a helper is as follows: The title help meet—completor is one that God bestowed upon a woman because he intended that she help her husband with **relationships**—his relationship with God and with others. No one knows a man as well as his wife. Nor does anyone have a capacity for commitment to a man like his wife **can** have. No one will be affected by a man's positive or negative relationship characteristics as will his wife. Negative characteristics affect a wife to such a degree that she **cannot** ignore them. So, making him aware of his negatives, for the purpose of developing solutions, is essential to her well-being as well as his.

The following is a partial list of common problems with which wives are struggling. Men definitely need to have their attention directed to these problems because they show a legitimate need for concern. Does your husband fit any of the following descriptions?

Yes   No

☐   ☐   **He does not communicate:** doesn't talk or express his thoughts about problems or anything else.

☐   ☐   **He is an unmotivated man:** lets his relationships and his house deteriorate; doesn't play with the children nor do things with his wife; mentally and/or physically isolates himself from family.

☐   ☐   **He is preoccupied with his own interests:** watches T.V. constantly; has projects he works on without stopping; is consumed with other activities such as hunting, fishing, golfing, or other types of sports, etc. (If he does invite his family along, he also invites his friends. Actually he is there with his friends.)

☐   ☐   **He makes fun of others:** teases wife, children, friends, etc.; tells ethnic jokes or jokes at other people's expense.

☐   ☐   **He is selfish with finances:** hoards money or spends money on self while making others feel as if they are draining the money supply unnecessarily; doesn't let wife know their financial picture; doesn't want anybody to spend any of **his** money.

☐   ☐   **He makes sexual demands:** disregards wife's feelings; creates within her feelings of disgust because she feels as though he is "using" her.

☐   ☐   **He puts wife down:** prefers his parents over his own family; prefers his children over his wife; prefers friends over family; or belittles wife in front of friends.

☐   ☐   **He has a bad temper:** family members are fearful of him.

☐   ☐   **He is a hypocritical Christian:** perfect in front of everyone else, but unwilling to pursue Christ-likeness at home.

This is only a partial list but it should serve as an example of wrong attitudes which men need to recognize and accept the responsibility for—to eliminate them from their lives. There are several ways to approach the problem of exposing these wrong attitudes. But at this point many wives might be trying to decide if they even want to pursue the idea of exposing their husband's wrong attitudes. I've asked many wives this question, "If your marriage continues down the same path it is headed right now ... because you don't want to 'rock the boat' ... what would you predict the future holds for your marriage? If that question is one you need to consider, also ponder these questions: Is pressing him for Christ-likeness worth the effort? Do you want things to keep going the way they are?

If you want to see things change, may I suggest three approaches for exposing and dealing with wrong attitudes and the reasoning behind them:

1. **RESORTING TO GOD**
   Pray for God's perspective in the particular situations you are facing. Seek out the most effective words, attitudes and circumstances for expressing your concerns. Ask God to help you know how to share your concerns or even if you should share them.

Nancy and I have come to some conclusions about the criteria to use in deciding when she should confront me with problems in my character or conduct.

... Is this an ongoing concern that causes her stress?

... Has she asked God to relieve her of that stress by distracting her through self-examination?

... Has she asked God to dismiss her of any responsibility towards carrying the burden of this problem?

If God still hasn't given her inner freedom after exploring these questions, then we both believe that it is correct for her to assume that God isn't going to release her from the turmoil of those problems until she comes to me with them. The next step is to then ask God to make clear in her mind what she needs to share with me.

If something is affecting your emotions, try to search your soul for understanding. Ask yourself, "**Why** is this affecting me?" You might even try fasting for awhile, to help soften your personality if necessary. If you can, get some faithful friends to join you in prayer and fasting. (See Esther 4:16) Then let your husband know that you are praying and fasting about something that you want to talk to him about. This will let him know that your concern is serious and important enough to make sure you include God. Maybe your concern before God will influence your husband's thinking enough to remind him of the need to guard his own response.

2. **RESORTING TO PERSONAL EFFORTS**
   Don't let "little" problems continue without sharing them because you think they are petty.

Little problems often have a way of becoming big problems. On the other hand don't assume too quickly that something you are suspicious about will definitely become a problem. If you let your suspicions **rule** your thinking you might find yourself becoming unnecessarily alarmed. You might find **yourself** developing conclusions about what the solution should be for something that is still just a suspicion. Talk your suspicions over with your husband.

I know that all of this requires effective communication with your husband and poor communication may be why you're facing some of these problems in the first place. In that event, part of the solution to your problems will include a stronger **focus** on the problem of poor communication.

In order to start sharing your heart effectively, let me remind you again that men operate mostly on the literal meaning of words. For example: If a wife were to say to her husband, "I don't **think** you love me!" He just might reply, "Well, you're wrong!"—because he **knows** that you are not as aware as he is about what he is actually **thinking!** And even though he may not actually be demonstrating love to you, he may still **think** he **is** loving. Since he does not naturally **think** like God, he probably is not measuring love from God's frame of reference (which is confirmed by his insensitive response to your statement). See I Cor. 13:4-8's report on love.

It is interesting to note how many husbands are not inclined to be inquisitive and **wonder why** their wives are making some of those negative statements. They don't seem to be curious enough to pursue a wife's emotionally charged statements and constructively ask questions. It doesn't occur to many men that those kinds of statements are motivated by something more than just the need for a woman to keep her vocal chords in working order. So, since men tend to function on the literal meaning of words, it might accomplish more if a wife would say, "I don't **feel** like you love me!" It's possible that he might believe it is his job to set your **thinking** straight by disputing or questioning the validity of your thinking, but let's hope he realizes that it's useless to dispute or question the validity of feelings. To genuinely care for a person requires that their feelings FIRST must be accepted and acknowledged—not as right or wrong, but as a fact.

If the things you want to discuss with your husband are spoken of in generalities then you should expect his responses to be in generalities. The more specific your comments are, the more specific will be his responses. For example: Having gotten the opportunity to talk to him let's suppose you say, "Our relationship needs improvement." That's pretty vague. He might say indifferently, "Whose doesn't?" His response reveals that he is unimpressed with your concern. However, if you were to be **more specific** and say, "I don't like the fact that we don't talk very much. Yesterday I turned on the cassette tape recorder when you came home just to see how much you talk with me. As I listened to the recording later, I counted only seven sentences by you in four hours. Would you like to listen to it?" Now you will get a specific conversational response from him!

When you talk to him about a specific situation or item, have as many facts with you as possible. Even little details are important. Have them written down for specific reference if you need to. This will help him face the facts, make a wiser decision, or respond intelligently, because he has more details to reflect upon.

Use descriptive "word pictures" to help him **see** what you're saying. The Proverbs, Psalms, and Jesus' parables are examples of word pictures. But tell him, "this is a word picture," or, "I'm going to exaggerate to make a point," or, "this is just an illustration."

Let him know that word pictures are a way of helping you convey your message to him. You may think . . . surely I don't have to actually say, "I'm just using a word picture here so I can convey what I'm feeling, do I? Anybody knows that, don't they?" Not necessarily. Remember, usually, a man will only take words literally; and if he does not know he has just been given a "word-picture," what you say might not make any sense to him. So in a man's mind, if your words sound exaggerated it will cause him to discredit your statements. So why run the risk of losing his attention or letting your omission of an explanation create a misunderstanding and cause your concerns to turn into an argument?

Using just a few words usually won't convey a word-picture to which he can relate. For example: "You're killing me!" is definitely a word-picture but it is not necessarily a word-picture that will have any impact. It leaves too much up to guess work if **he** has to do the interpreting. He know's he's not literally killing you. However, if you say, "I feel like you care so little for me that if I were on a deserted road and someone was chasing me trying to kill me and you found out, you wouldn't care enough to come and help me. You're so tied up in yourself (or your work, etc.) you don't have time for anything or anyone else. You may not like to hear that, but that's how I feel!" Now that's a word picture!

That kind of word picture will stir feelings within your husband too. Even though he may not be in touch with them, your husband does have feelings. Try to notice times when he is experiencing feelings; try to draw **his** attention to them. Somehow try to capture the feelings he's experiencing at a given moment **in your memory.** Then later, as you are trying to convey to him how he is making you feel, remind him of those feelings he had earlier and see if you can thereby get him to better identify with the feelings that you are experiencing now.

Even though discussions about relationship problems are difficult, try to establish a relaxed atmosphere if at all possible. Most of the time it's best to discuss a problem when you're not right in the middle of it . . . wait until later. And yes, I do realize that discussing it later may still result in your being right in the "middle of it" again.

If you've decided to pursue a solution for your problems

this far, you may also have to count the cost and decide whether you are willing to go one step further. If your husband continues to act as though he is honorable and self-rightous in front of others, yet continues to be irresponsible, abusive or uninterested in seeking help, there is more that can be done.

3. **RESORTING TO HELP FROM OTHERS**
   I already know that the following may be viewed by some as being manipulative. But it should not be thought of as scheming or manipulative when, to accomplish righteousness, it's necessary to set up the circumstances that create accountability. The word manipulation is often a scare word used by men to get women "back-in-line." **That's** manipulation!

> The word manipulation is not to be used only in a negative sense. Should manipulation be considered in a negative sense if you maneuver a person into receiving a benefit? If you could maneuver someone into a position of being eligible to receive $10,000 ... would that be negative? If a wife can help her husband enjoy the benefits of a more Christ-centered relationship, is that wrong? With that in mind, is it wrong to be constructively honest?

At what point should a wife seek to make her husband accountable before others? When the first two steps we've mentioned prove fruitless. The tendency in most wives though is to keep postponing drastic measures in hopes that their situation will change...in time. I believe Matthew 18:15, 16 is also applicable to marriages. After trying to communicate with your husband, if he doesn't seem as though he is motivated to care, let him know that you are going to take further steps which include sharing specifics about your problems with his parents (especially if his parents are scripturally sound). If sharing with his parents is not possible, or if you feel it is preferable, you may find that he would likely be more motivated to change if you were to go to his Christian friends. If you can't get satisfaction by going to them ... then go to your church's leadership.

> Don't be surprised though, if you discover that the men you approach about your husband's offenses are not only **un**willing to help, but that they might be offending their wives similarly. They may turn against you in support of your husband! Remember ... we're living in a time when men will boastfully admit they don't know how to understand women, which is a violation of I Peter 3:7 ... *"In the same way, you married men should live considerately with your wives, with an* **intelligent recognition** *of the marriage relationship,* **honoring** *the women ..."* (AMP Bible)

You must keep two things in mind if you decide to follow this path:

   1. **Most men don't respond to marriage relationship needs until the pressure of problems force them to.** I'm convinced that men coined the phrase, "You only grease the wheel that squeaks." In other words ... when the pressures of life force a man to do something, then he does it. Preventive

maintenance does not seem to be a recognized need in the **marriage community.** Should it be a standard policy that we wait for the average husband to become **self-**motivated—waiting for him to seek mutually beneficial solutions when facing marriage problems? If that were the only policy, in too many cases there would be no solution coming. Evidence shows that in most situations, at best, we would be in for an unnecessarily long wait. With little research, we discover that the "average Christian" marriage in America is in **bad** shape—if we compare it with God's standards. It's awful that this is the case. That's why exposing a husband's wrong attitudes and actions **specifically** in front of his friends is often exactly the kind of pressure a husband needs to get him interested in changing. Because so many men are unmotivated to make their marriage a showpiece I have further bad news: If your marriage has reached the typical condition, exposing the facts about your marriage will probably prove embarrassing to both of you before he will be motivated. Don't expect him to thank you for this "helpful" motivation either.

2. **Expect this method to take a lot of time and to be an immense source of pressure on you too. You must have a commitment to seeing it through—or don't even start it.** Also, make it a part of your honesty with others to give good reports of his efforts to change (as he does change) or even when his efforts show that he is trying hard to change.

There is sufficient scriptural precedent for publicly holding men accountable, even by women. If you're going to be calculating . . . let it be for righteousness. The following are examples of women who held men accountable:

... Esther, acting under the advice of her former guardian (without consulting her husband) devised a plan that cost a high-ranking official his life. (Esther 2:10-6:10)

... The daughter-in-law of Judah successfully managed to publicly hold her father-in-law accountable for not being obedient to scripture, nor following his own rules and keeping his word to her. (Gen. 38:1-26)

... Nathan, the prophet of God, set up a situation to trap even the king (David) into deciding his own punishment for sinfulness. (II Sam. 12:1-10)

... Paul scolded Peter for his preferential treatment of the Jews. (Gal. 2:11-14)

... A woman who was ill-treated by her brother-in-law had him brought before the authorities where he was publicly disgraced as she was required to spit in his face as part of his punishment. (Deut. 25:5-10)

Now after all of that guidance I would be negligent if I did not add this: If you found yourself faced with reliable and convicting evidence showing you how you had been offensive and had severely damaged someone's emotions, you probably would be reduced to shame, tears, and regrets, etc., right? Not necessarily so for men though. The reasons why men are not usually as emotionally affected when confronted can vary from man to man. Here are some of the reasons:

• Negative circumstances in his early childhood may have hurt him so badly that he forced himself to hide his own emotions. He may have totally blocked out his capacity to relate to another person; so much so, that it may take years and years to restore his own emotions to their normal capacity in order that he might be able to relate to you.

• Out of pure stubbornness, pride may make him resist admitting that he has been wrong.

• He won't admit he's been wrong and you've been right

because he thinks that that kind of confession is not consistent with a strong leader; only a weakling would admit to being wrong. To him, it would be the same as relinquishing his role as 'boss'.

• He really doesn't care about what you or God thinks. He may never have had to face "living out" the Christian life, especially the part that talks about focusing on his own shortcomings first (his attitudes might well generate questions about the reality of his "Christianity").

There are many more reasons, but none of them offer a legitimate excuse for continuing to be emotionally irresponsible, and behaving in an unChrist-like way.

It may take some serious circumstances to capture your husband's attention and get him to submit his will to God. With this goal in mind—that your husband submit himself to God in order that you both may have a God-centered marriage—are you prepared to go through the difficult experiences which God might set in motion to get your husband to surrender?

In spite of all we've just mentioned, neither you nor I, nor anyone else can **force** your husband to desire Christlikeness. We can only try to be channels through which God might reach him . . . and that **can** happen! There are men who are waking up, realizing it is possible to actually develop the capacity to understand their wives. In a caring way, they are learning how to minister to their wives. They are enjoying their marriage and actually fulfilling the admonition of I Peter 3:7 . . . thereby setting their wives free to be the persons God designed them to be; not the persons they felt they had to be in order to pacify their husbands.

CHAPTER NINE

IS HIS KIND OF LOVE KILLING YOU?

I know of so many cases where a husband would say he loves his wife. But his wife would say, "if you call that love, then please don't love me anymore."

If a man basically thinks on a 'mechanical' plane then quite naturally he will tend to feel much more comfortable responding to life mechanically. Since his mind (not his heart) is where he does most of his reasoning, he can easily think that he is an expert when it comes to mechanically managing his home. It is quite natural for most men to feel comfortable controlling or managing their own life; and since his marriage or his family are a part of what he considers to be **his** life, he will want to manage and control them. Many men tend to think they are adequate or accomplished when **they** are the manager or controller of their marriage. Put another way, many men can feel irresponsible and as if they are failing in their duties if they **do not** manage and control their marriage.

When it comes to a man's deepest interpretation of the terms manage/control, I think his instinctive definition would have to include his requiring ABSOLUTE, UNQUESTIONING OBEDIENCE. I believe there is good reason for a man to have that instinctive outlook when it comes to his family: protection! I also think that as a man wants that type of response from his family for their benefit and protection (even if it means his own death), God also wants that type of response from a man ... for that man's benefit and protection. But too many men are letting that noble instinct be perverted by SELFISHNESS.

Let me give a personal illustration which I think shows the value of that instinctive need for absolute, unquestioning obedience. When my daughter Sarah was about eight years old, she, Nancy, and I were driving on a country road near a small river. We saw a piece of property for sale and thought it would be fun to look at. We stopped and got out of the car. There was a country home or small farm not too far away, maybe the distance of a football field. Nancy wasn't too far away from the car but Sarah and I were a good 200 feet away when all of a sudden we all saw two big dogs racing towards us barking, growling, and viciously baring their teeth. They had come up on us so fast that Sarah and I could not have made it back to the car in time to escape the dogs. Nancy, who was nearer to the car, was either screaming or crying (I can't remember which for sure) wanting to get into the car but not wanting to leave us outside alone. Sarah started screaming and running towards the car. There was about 30 feet between Sarah and I and it looked as though the dogs had decided she was the one to go after. Keeping an eye on the dogs, I caught up with Sarah, grabbed her and said in a loud, firm and demanding voice, "DO NOT RUN. NO MATTER WHAT HAPPENS, YOU KEEP ME BETWEEN YOU AND THE DOGS!" I crouched with my knees bent for flexibility. Then I stretched out my arms to create a larger image and to keep them free in case of attack. Facing the dogs, I stood still. My mind imagined the battle plan: "No matter what the cost, get a hold of the bottom jaw, then break it." My mind examined the cost: There was going to be a lot of blood and flesh that would need to be put back together. But not even for a second was all that cause to run or save myself. No cost was too great to keep Sarah from being hurt. The dogs charged to within about 15 feet of us and stopped, still growling and snarling, the dogs ears were back. They crouched, waiting and watching, I felt like I had the advantage now! However, I knew I could not walk away yet . . . that might let them think they could still attack. Instead I started slowly advancing, making a noise like I was growling or warning them. They backed up a little. When they did, I stopped, giving them a chance to retreat. They slowly started to turn, keeping an eye on me. It was over. Sarah had been absolutely, unquestioningly obedient ... avoiding complications.

There was never even a question in my mind about facing this problem. It was all instinctive and those God-given instincts are for physical survival. But when it comes to spiritual survival (in relationships), I need maximum help.

I think that almost every husband or father would be able to say, "If that were me, I would have done the same thing!" And that's why it's confusing to a man when he knows that those are the attitudes of his heart and yet his wife or family tells him that they do not feel like he loves them. But, if a man doesn't have a scriptural perspective which includes **mutually honoring** his spouse, he won't think in terms of honoring **her** God-given instincts about relationships. He will continue to do what comes naturally to most men: **managing and controlling** his wife and family with unconsciously selfish motives. And instead of his family feeling loved, they will feel unloved.

This brings us to ... FACT #8 ... **Most men think that survival is based only on protecting the body.** The idea of the emotions or spirit needing protection is relatively unheard of. When hearing the term, "Survival of the Fittest", I'm sure almost all men would relate it to physical survival and not spiritual survival. Maybe that's why, when Jesus sent the disciples out into the world to spread the Gospel, He drew their attention to that difference: Don't fear anything that is a threat to your physical life. Rather fear that which will destroy your spiritual life. (Matt. 10:28)

A man managing his family improperly will not convey love to his family: Instead he will experience tension and disharmony in his home. He may feel more comfortable at work and may experience so much more success at his job that he will become a work-aholic. If your husband is a work-aholic don't assume that you and the children are driving him there. Furthermore, if being around his home causes him discomfort, don't conclude that you are the source of his discomfort.

Since men basically are not very capable or expert when it comes to relationships, they will tend to avoid that area (home) where their instinctive abilities are lacking and where that lack of skill stands out. Staying away because he feels inadequate is not something a man consciously thinks about, though; it is felt in his subconscious and is something he will subconsciously act upon. A simplified expression of this problem would look like this:

... If he feels good, adequate, or comfortable about the demands of work ... then he will want to be there. He will keep working.

...If he feels lousy, **in**adequate, or **un**comfortable about the demands of relationships ... then he will want to stay away from them. He will avoid that relationship.

Even excessively working around his own house can be an escape for him. But keep in mind that most men don't plan on working excessively to avoid the requirements of a relationship. They just **instinctively** focus on work because it's easier, therefore more enjoyable—thus avoiding the uncomfortable feelings caused from **sensing** their relationship inadequacies. Again, you or the family did **not cause** his "work-aholism." If he had the necessary understanding of and the ability to successfully handle relationships, he would enjoy being around that success too.

"For where your treasure is, there will your heart be also." (Matthew 6:21 KJV)

Here are some typical examples of naturally instinctive, male, "mechanical" thinking: You and your husband are hiking in the Arizona desert. You're going through a rocky area with slow-rolling hills. Your walk leads you to a small chasm or crack across your path. There is a four foot space or gap between the ledge you're on and the ledge across from you. As you and your husband approach this gap, your husband might simply, without hesitation, jump across it.

> Often due to the God-given **physical** survival instincts, a man's mind **will have automatically computed** (as he approached the gap and while he's making the jump) such things as: where should I place my feet when I land; what are the conditions of both surfaces; will I slip if it's gravelly or wet; how much slippage should I allow for; how much supportive strength will I need to devote to my ankles, legs, etc. for take-off and landing.

Then there's a wife's response: It's not usually based on the instinctive capacity to calculate the conditions for physical survival. Most often her instincts are based on the capacity to calculate the conditions for emotional-spiritual survival. In a situation like this (trail-blazing) a woman will usually demonstrate cautious hesitation. The average wife would experience pressure, especially if her husband was applying pressure and trying to coax her with statements like, "Go ahead and jump! Come on! It's easy!" but you find it's not so easy for you; you don't naturally think mechanically. You wonder if it's really possible for you to make it even though you saw him do it.

To further illustrate the contrast in responses to life based on God-given differences, consider the following: Late one night, you and your family are returning home on a remote country road; your husband is driving. The car starts acting up. You become alarmed and excitedly ask, "What's wrong?" Not only does he not answer you, but you get the distinct feeling that he is angry at you for bothering him with questions. Why? because talking to you, at this point, is a distraction and an inconvenience. Why? Because his mind has become absorbed by the car. In his mind he is

mechanically trying to locate the problem so he can mentally start "working" on the car. His survival juices are flowing. He probably is mentally trying to discover, through a process of elimination, what the problem is and he doesn't want to stop "working" to talk. What are you doing in the meantime? Worrying about the effects of a broken down car upon your family. If the car stops, will your husband have to go for help? That means, since it's late at night and the kids are sleeping, you can't go with him. Therefore you will have to stay in the car with the kids. Alone! Are you and the kids going to be safe, etc.? Your survival juices are flowing too. But each of you is focusing on different survival needs. Both are valuable instincts.

This type of situation can be even more irritating if you've already told him that the car was acting up and he seemed to ignore your warning. Although he naturally thinks "mechanically" and feels more comfortable in that mode, a husband hasn't been given the freedom by God to exclusively remain in that mode. A husband must examine himself: "Am I illustrating the capacity to understand and lovingly relate to my wife as Christ does?"

> *"For this reason I kneel before the Father, from whom his whole family in heaven and on earth derives its name. I pray that out of His glorious riches* **He may strengthen you** *with power* **through His Spirit in your inner being,** *so* **that Christ may dwell in your hearts** *through faith. And I pray that you, being rooted and established in love, may have power, together with the saints, to grasp how wide and long and big and deep is the love of Christ, and* **to know this love that surpasses knowledge** *- that you may be filled to the measure of all the fullness of God." (Eph. 3:14-19 NIV) "Husbands, love your wives,* **just as Christ loved** *the church . . ." (Eph. 5:25 NIV)*

I pray that more and more men will learn the value of letting their wives help them develop emotional/spiritual survival instincts. The world needs more examples of men who, as a natural response, illustrate the love of Christ to their wives because it's their nature to love in a way that fulfills their wives, instead of killing them!

CHAPTER TEN

IS A WIFE MORE AWARE OF HER HUSBAND'S HEART THAN HE IS?

We are living in a world that has removed itself far from God. I've wondered if anything short of Christ's return and the establishment of His kingdom will cause the hearts of even many who call themselves Christian to turn loose of their ungodliness. We need to stop trying to justify our disobedience and stop making excuses for our sin. It seems like we've been drawn down so low—so far away from God—the question must be asked, "Do we even come close; are we really presenting ourselves as **"living epistles, so known and so read by all men"** as we are challenged to be in II Cor. 3:2?

While reflecting on that, let me illustrate my point about excusing our disobedience. Men are supposed to be providing the type of Christian leadership that would cause a wife to rejoice at submitting to that leadership. Wives should have the confidence that submitting to their husbands is as though submitting to Christ. At this juncture it is necessary to point out that **submission is an act of freedom.** If there is no choice, then submission is not the consideration. You are then dealing with slavery or servitude, i.e., obedience to a command.

Many men have been so extremely out of line with God's concepts about marriage that even discovering where to start correcting those mistakes is a problem. It's difficult for them to know where to begin realigning those false perspectives that so badly hinder their marriages. Keeping their wives from experiencing the freedom that submission requires—in order for it to be genuine submission.

And yet it is becoming clearer and clearer (to even the non-Christian world) that women generally have a keener, more natural understanding of relationships than men do. You would think then, that husbands would show appreciation and be anxious to benefit from that expertise in women. You would think we would realize that a wife's knowledge of relationships is very important to a man and that it would even help him gain a better understanding of his role as a husband. And yet most men are not excited about learning from their wives like they should be. If women do have a better understanding about the spirit of relationships, and men are willing to recognize their need to improve, then an important question that needs to be asked is: Will women **help men** or **resent men?**

Wives have suffered much under the reign of husbands because of men's ignorance about relationships. But that wouldn't have to be the case if more men would be willing to investigate the possibilities or realities of the following:

FACT #9 . . . **A wife is usually much more in touch with her husband's spirit than he is.** We really need to know how that is possible! Too many men don't even have the slightest idea of what the spirit of a person is. Let me quickly re-identify the spirit: It is the inner person.

Here's the simplest way I have of explaining it. When a woman says to her husband, "You don't love me!" A husband's response will probably be, "I do too!"

She will probably insist, "No, you don't!"

His reaction will probably sound like this, "Don't tell me I don't love you, 'cause I know I do!"

Because he is not listening to her spirit she will try to explain, "You don't love **me,** you just love **my body!**"

Many a husband hearing this will think that this is **very strange talk.** The average husband won't be able to identify with what his wife is saying!!

But the "me" she is talking about when she says, "You don't love **me**," is her inner-self, **her spirit.**

Every person has a spirit. Christians are supposed to let God's Spirit direct their spirit.

> "Howbeit when He, **the Spirit** of truth is come, **He will guide you** into all truth." (John 16:13 KJV)
> ". . . and no one can really say, Jesus is my Lord, except by and under the power and influence of the Holy Spirit." (I Cor. 12:3b AMP Bible)

That's one of the aspects involved in our becoming spiritually more mature: we become more receptive to God's Spirit directing our spirit. In order for that to become a reality, we men must develop an awareness of the fact that we do have a spirit. Ordinarily the fact that we (men) have a spirit will not occur to us; and if we are not alert to our own spirit, there will not likely be a sensitivity in our spirit which would allow us to cooperate with God's Spirit. Without the leadership of God's spirit, our spirit will not become more and more mature.

An aspect of learning about the reality of the spirit involves getting in touch with the emotions. Emotions help identify the condition of a person's spirit. I am convinced that the Scriptures reveal to us that a person's emotions are the way to measure or evaluate the condition of a person's spirit. Emotions give us the ability to measure the effects of a given situation or set of circumstances upon a person's spirit at any given moment. Proverbs 15:13 says:

> "A happy **heart** (spirit/inner-person) makes the face **cheerful** (emotions: evidence of the condition of the spirit)." Parenthesis mine.

Let me explain this belief with a practical illustration. Your family is going to take a restful trip to the mountains for a whole week, alone. As a wife and mother, your spirit or inner-person knows that this special time will be valuable for the family. It will give the whole family time to build relationships and a chance to build meaningful memories. Your husband will have a chance to get away from work. You both will be free to spend some special time with the kids. As you imagine all the good possibilities you feel very pleased and happy ... those are emotions. Those emotions reveal how your spirit/inner-self feels about this trip.

You're getting ready to go ... there's a lot of preparation. It's physically tiring, but you don't mind because your spirit/inner-person knows how important this get-away is. But you're also worried (an emotion) about your husband's lack of patience (his emotions about all this). Because it's a break from his normal routine, you sense his spirit/inner-person is struggling. It's difficult for most men to see the spirits of each person and recognize the value of this occasion for their spirits. He can't seem to stop thinking about his work and all of its unmet demands. Maybe he's impatient because of last minute delays—he wants to get on the road. He's getting up-tight and frustrated (his inner-self is not relating to the spirit of the occasion). Because you sense his explosiveness, you try to keep the hyper-excited kids under control so he won't get angry (an emotion based on his spirit's frustration over the demands of an event that requires involvement on a spirit-to-spirit level).

Of the husband or wife, which one do you think is being more influenced by the effects of emotions; displaying a greater awareness of and concern for each individual's spirit?

> It's too bad that the husband in this story is not more in tune with the fact that each of his family members has a spirit. Then he would see this as a valuable time for their spirits to be bound together. Knowing that he was building family security would help him overcome his anger. He should know that job-related problems, especially at this time, should not take priority over the spirits of his family members. But too often, men are not aware that their family members even have a spirit—that each human being has a spirit.

See how each person in a given situation has emotional responses. And **each emotion** is a reflection of how your spirit/inner-person is being affected by **each situation.** Now you see why the world is such a mess. Almost everything we do at one point or another will affect relationships (especially in families) and relationships must experience emotions. But the world is full of men who don't have a clue about the importance of a **person's spirit;** men who place little value on **people's emotions**—both of which are key components for meaningful relationships.

The example I just used also disproves a common philosophy that says: "The responsibility for the atmosphere in the home rests upon the wife." That's a convenient philosophy for men to have developed and one which most men find easy to accept. But I don't think it lines up with the facts.

For example, if everybody in the family is in a good mood and the father comes home in a bad mood, watch what happens to the atmosphere in that home. Even though the mother's composure was calm before he came upon the scene and even though she's trying as hard as she can to maintain the family's positive spirit, his negative disposition will still cause disharmony, maybe even havoc. On the other hand, if everybody is in a bad mood, and dad comes home in a good mood, he will **positively** affect the whole family if he will keep his composure.

I've discovered that Nancy actually knows my disposition better than I do. Over the years, she has carefully observed me. She has mentally charted my character, my habits, my emotions . . . my spirit. Since she is more alert to the spirit of family members, the atmosphere in the home and the relationship between us, a negative atmosphere usually has a much more serious affect on her than it does on me. Because of my past ignorance about the spirit of a person, she has had to try to be the spiritual leader in our home in order to keep harmony. Because she has studied me, she can tell by my walk, but the way I drive, by the way I breathe, etc., what my temperament is at that moment. Nancy knows me better than I know myself in many areas of my life. That enables her to see, often long before I do, when I'm beginning to get off track in my quest for Christ-likeness. She sees when I'm starting back into my old ways. If **I really value Nancy** and her ability to perceive my tendencies that well, it can be quite an advantage for me . . . she can actually warn me **before** I get too far off track or cause to much grief, etc.

No longer do I have to wait until I've become so offensive to God and everyone else that they can hardly stand me before I also become aware of my negative disposition.

I can make corrections sooner. But before Nancy will feel secure enough to let me know ahead of time how offensive I'm being, I've got to reassure her. She has to feel secure in the knowledge that I really do appreciate her help. **She** must **know** that her relationship with me **is safe** before she feels the freedom to be that honest with me—before she can be honest enough to tell me that I have **started** to head off in a wrong direction.

> If a husband is basically not aware of, or familiar with his own spirit, his spirit cannot be mature. An immature spirit will have immature attitudes. The problems are numerous when wives sense the immature attitudes of their husband's spirit and **try to cope** with that lack of spiritual leadership.

DISHONESTY IN COMMUNICATION

In opposition to the positive attitudes previously given, let me give you some examples of how wives (sensing their husband's negative spirits) can be dishonest because they're trying to avoid conflict. This dishonesty will not serve the desired purpose of bringing harmony and happiness, however. Most husbands don't recognize when their wives sacrifice their consciences. Nor will they recognize the noble motivation of their desire to avoid a conflict. On the contrary, most husbands will be oblivious to the fact that their wives do not feel the freedom to be honest with them. Rather, the average husband will believe and accept his wife's report even though it is a dishonest representation. Let me explain.

On occasion we have used a form for applicants who wish to participate in our workshops and discipleship programs. On it there is a question designed to find out the condition of their marriage?

Question: What would you say is the overall condition of your marriage?

Wife: □ Good   □ Fair   □ Poor   □ Serious
Husband   □ Good   □ Fair   □ Poor   □ Serious

I remember one wife filled out the form in ink (making it uneraseable) and checked the box for 'Serious'. Then she handed the form to her husband to check the box for the husband's response. He saw what his wife had marked and was very upset. Without too many words, but alot of negative facial expressions, she got his message: he was rejecting her and her evaluation of their marriage. So she scratched out 'serious' and moved her 'X' to the "Fair" box which matched his mark of evaluation and thereby she was able to meet with his approval!

Later, looking over their form and noticing the scratched out box, I guessed what probably had happened. Out of concern, I sought her out for an explanation. After she confirmed my suspicions I said to her, "Do you know that when you made that change on the form, you convinced your husband that you were wrong and he was right? He thinks you 're-evaluated' your opinion, recognized 'your error' and made your mark in the 'correct' box? Now he's convinced that you, too, **believe** as he does and everything is fine! Do you realize that's what has taken place?"

With defeat and frustration in her voice she said, "I didn't want to hurt his feelings and cause a scene in front of everybody. It just didn't seem **that** important to me . . . so I changed it."

But it **is VERY** important! He is not having to face reality and make a decision about his responsibility as a Christian husband to care for his wife. Do you think he recognized and valued her desire to avoid conflict? Do you think her dishonesty brought her the desired benefit of **building** their relationship?

Later on in life, some of these defeated wives feel like they can't handle anymore of their husband's offenses so they start packing a suitcase. Each husband who has come upon this scene—who is standing there watching in confusion asks, "What's wrong!?!?!" And his wife can't believe that he is honestly wondering what is wrong!

Wives think they are letting their husbands know of their discontent with messages that seem very clear to them. A wife thinks the message is real clear when she marks the box "Serious." It's not unusual for a wife to mistakenly believe that even though her husband made her change her mark in that box when he put pressure on her, he still realizes what she **really feels.** But most of the signals that a wife might give which she thinks will be a clear indication of dissatisfaction with her husband are too subtle for most men. And the more you let him be "fooled" because you are resorting to "hints," or hoping he will "pick up" the messages you're "dropping," the more calloused he will become to the truth!

DECEPTION IN COMMUNICATION

In most marriages deception is hiding behind the flag of truce. For example:

It's vacation time. You live in California. You want to visit his aging parents in Virginia; he wants to go to Disneyland. He really raises a fuss. Some of his arguments are even legitimate, like . . . the **kids** won't have as much fun; we **did** visit them last vacation; Disneyland is **closer;** it **won't** cost as much, etc. Even though you haven't changed your mind and deep down inside you really feel you shouldn't, you give in. You surrender with words like, "Yeah, **I guess you're right!"**

But that wasn't honest. To be honest you should have said something like this, "I really don't agree with you. I think we should take advantage of the time while your parents are still around. The children should be able to enjoy memories of their grandparents, especially since your parents won't be around forever and Disneyland probably will. However, I'm going to given in and go along with your wishes because your anger and selfishness is putting pressure on me. So even though I'm giving in to what you want, don't think later that I agreed with your decision." But you didn't say that! Instead you said, "I guess you're right."

Now a year later it's vacation time again and you say, "How about **this year** we do something **I** want to do?" And he reacts, "Wait a minute; last year **you wanted** to go to Disneyland, **too.** You said I was right! **You agreed** that it was best! Don't try to act like I twisted your arm!"

That's what your husband heard!! Almost any husband would hear the same thing: **You wanted** to do it also!!

MANIPULATION IN COMMUNICATION

Confused communication is most often the chief trouble-maker in conflicts between a husband and wife. And more often than not the husband is going to get his way. So the average wife starts to think that her husband is very selfish and probably won't even consider the family's needs or her desires. Because they are not working as a team, a wife may conclude that if her or other family member's desires or concerns are going to be fulfilled, she will have to start scheming. So maneuvering her husband is not out of the question. Wives recognize their physical and emotional **powerlessness** when it comes to confronting their husbands. Many a wife might conclude upon determining the need and then considering the time schedule, what kind of plan she must put into action. Then she will begin to start maneuvering her husband, far in advance of the needs she has decided should be met. Many a wife realizes that if there's something she is **wishing for**, she will have to start manipulating; otherwise she **knows what to expect** . . . don't you?

I think the aforementioned can easily be seen as additional evidence that wives really can read and anticipate husbands better than husbands can read and anticipate themselves. I think it shows how a wife can accurately predict her husband's characteristically negative responses even though a husband doesn't recognize he has predictable negative characteristics.

SIDE-TRACKING IN COMMUNICATION

Let me point out the nature of this problem ahead of time so you can watch it as it unfolds in the illustration.

A wife wants to talk with her husband; there is something

she needs to discuss. She therefore starts the discussion with a specific concern—which we will call her "Point A". But her husband isn't in the habit of listening to her. He has not illustrated that he wants to discover what wave length she's on. So when she presents her "Point A" to her husband, he reflects on **her words** from **his point of view.** It's not unusual for him to **hear** her saying something **entirely different** from what **she was actually** saying. We'll call what **he thinks** she is saying but, is actually a totally **different subject,** his "Point B." Now he launches into an in-depth discussion with her about **his** "Point B." And she finds herself totally caught up in **his** discussion. She doesn't even get to continue talking about her concern . . . "Point A." It got lost in the argument that was the result of his misunderstanding. He never even knew what she was saying.

Here's the illustration: This wife has felt for a long time that she is unimportant to her husband. Even though they live in the same house their lives are separated; they both occupy their free time with independent activities. This evening was typical. They both were passing time, doing their own thing. The phone rang. The wife picked it up. It was for him. It was his unit of the National Guard. They called because they had something they wanted him to do . . . they were really depending on him . . . could they count on him to take care of this special request they were making of him? His phone conversation revealed that he was very enthusiastic about having this opportunity to serve,— knowing that they needed him. By the time he hung up the phone he sounded very excited. She asked him a simple question that clearly revealed **her concern** . . . "Point A," "Why don't you get **as enthusiastic** about **taking care of the needs of our relationship** as you do about the National Guard?" ("Point A": His lack of enthusiasm about their marriage.)

His response: "Why do you **hate the Guard** so much?" (There's **his** "Point B": what he determines is her jealousy towards the National Guard.) Does she draw him back to "Point A?" No! She says, "I don't hate the Guard!" (Now starts the emotionally draining—totally erroneous debate.)

He responds, "Yes, you do. You're always putting down the Guard or trying to make me choose between it and you!"

She defends herself, "No, I'm not! I know you enjoy the Guard. I wouldn't want to do that to you."

He accuses, "Well, why-da-ya always act like you want me to get out of it then?" And on and on it goes.

Did he realize what she was really trying to say? Does he realize what he did? On both counts . . . no!

Watch and see how many times you find yourself getting drawn back into this same type of confrontation. Notice how easy it is to lose track of your original "Point A".

Why do you suppose so many wives spend so much time talking with **a friend** on the phone? **The friend understands her!**

Even though most women sense the marriage going sour (because of inadequate spiritual leadership) long before most men do, they amaze me with their capacity to keep hoping. Why does it amaze me? Because if they see it sooner, that also means that they will have been feeling the pain of a bad relationship sooner. I've seen thousands of wives who were hurting **so** badly and each husband was absolutely oblivious to the destruction that was going on right under his nose. If I had a dollar for every man that I've heard say, "My wife is leaving me and I don't know why!?" I'd be a rich man!

Sensing the character of her husband's spirit, often more clearly than her husband does, many a wife tries to convince her husband that **they** need help to keep their marriage from disaster. Too often a husband will **prove** that his wife **is** more in touch with his spirit than he is with this kind of reply, "**I** don't need any help! If you think something is wrong, that's **your** problem. So you **must be** the one who needs help!"

Can you see how so many different types of marriage problems develop and how it takes so much effort to untangle them?

CHAPTER ELEVEN

COULD ANYONE HAVE TOLD YOU?

The following letter was received by a bewildered husband*. Have you ever written or thought about writing this kind of letter?

Dear Wayne,

I am writing this because I do not want to put either of us through anymore than we have already been through and writing will let us avoid a face-to-face trial. Surely we both realize that our life together has been over for some time and it doesn't seem as if there is enough left to even try to rebuild it.

At his point our trying to stay together is making all of us unhappier by the minute. I've thought alot about our situation. In fact, that's all I've thought about for six months, and I've decided that I should move out. It was not my first choice, but nothing else seems worthwhile considering!

I've left a letter for each of the children. I trust that you will give it to them. I know they will be upset, but I am trying to save everyone the trauma of trying to patch up a bad situation and the strain of living in one. I love the children very much and I know I will never make another decision that has been as painful as this one. I only hope that they will understand—if not now—maybe later. I hope they will not hate me so much that they will not want to stay in touch with me, and that they will want to see as much of me as school, etc. allows.

I do not want anything from you.

I have already filed the papers for a divorce. They need only be signed and returned. I've paid all the fees, so there won't be anything for you to be concerned with.

This brown folder contains birth certificates, death records, car titles, and telephone numbers. I've added your name to my bank checking account,

(*Used by permission and the names have been changed.)

because of the insurance automatic withdrawal and you will receive new checks and a Visa card in the mail soon. If this account is not convenient you can close it out. I left it open because it is the one with the insurance and the one we have been using. You may sign your name to my remaining checks and cash them at the bank until the new printed ones arrive.

I am deeply sorry for the way things have washed out for us. I never dreamed 22 years ago that things could ever end like this. I hope that this will in some way lift a burden from you and allow you to go on with your life and to some day be happy.

Joan

Do you suppose that any woman ever gets married to a man and plans on this type of ending? Of course not! No one does, but it happens. Why?

This letter shows that she lived with this situation for years and that she tolerated it as long as she felt she could, then **planned** her escape for at least six months before letting him know about it. How in the world could things get that bad and **he not even know it?** Why didn't he recognize the signs? Please excuse these harsh sounding words, but, the truth of the matter is that he didn't realize what was taking place right under his nose because he is spiritually blind, deaf and ignorant!

Let me introduce here ... FACT #10 ... **Marriage relationships, directed by natural-to-human tendencies (without God's direction) will generally get worse.**

It seems as though most women let their emotions govern them when it comes to evaluating **the man** they've decided is "Mr. Right."

I haven't known of too many women who have asked other people (friends, relatives, etc.) to get to know the man they are letting into their heart in order to help them evaluate him (his character) before marriage. It seems like most of the time women react to warnings from others (especially parents) instead of valuing the concerns expressed **in their own behalf.** Too often women think, "They don't really know him like I do!" The real facts are, however, that other people are not letting their emotions influence and control their conclusions. Nor are other people bound as this woman is: She may want what she wants more than she wants what's best! Many, many women are struggling with the natural-to-woman instinct which compels them to seek out **that one to whom she can give her heart.** That instinct is so strong that **the fear of not having** that **special person** to whom **she also is special** is very powerful and able to dominate many a woman's emotions. The desire to have someone she can join in a life-long commitment is highly instinctive and very strong. Yet most women don't seem to be aware of how much it can control them. It often blinds women to reality. They can make an **intense** commitment to a man and not even realize that he hasn't made a commitment to her that is even close to the commitment she has made. And to often NO ONE CAN TELL HER! This blindness in women causes them to set themselves up for grief—especially when they assume the following ideas are facts:

• **After we're married, he will care for my inner-most needs because he will be my husband.** No so! Men don't naturally know how to care for the inner-most needs of a woman. Even those men you might label as "Mister Wonderful" don't always know how to actually understand the mind of a woman. A man's thoughfulness before marriage is not proof that he understands relationships. The attentive ways of most men before marriage are centered around the idea of "winning" the woman—making a conquest—making her his!

• **Things will improve after marriage.** Not so! In fact, if you don't expect, after marriage, that at least three times as many disagreeable characteristics or circumstances are going to be revealed, you're going to be in for a big surprise. Often people are drawn to each other because of opposites. For example:

A. She's talkative—he's a listener.

B. He's aggressive—she's a 'wallflower'.

C. He's moody—she's sympathetic, etc.

Once they're married, those personality opposites are going to be, more frequently, in closer contact with each other. Demands are going to be made upon each other as husband and wife that wouldn't even occur to a single person (sexual demands, sharing personal-private quarters, personal tastes, etc.). The occasions that lend themselves to offenses are simply going to present themselves more frequently. Then those opposites that attracted, start irritating:

A. She never stops talking—he never enters into conversations.

B. He dominates her life—she won't get involved in matters.

C. He's so depressed—she's always nagging him to get up and get going.

• **He will take more responsibility and be less selfish after marriage.** No so! You should realize that many men instinctively believe that when a man gets married he is **the** boss. If he's the boss . . . then she is not the boss! The one who is not the boss is often thought to be the one who is supposed to wait on the boss, hand-and-foot. Too many men operate on this attitude: I've obtained a woman and it's her responsibility to make me the center of her life.

Most women do not recognize the seriousness of the need to honestly evaluate men. They do not tend to believe that "their man" is a **normal** man, **without** normal-to-God attitudes and reflections towards women.

Before marriage, if you see areas in "your man's" life that definitely need to change, remember this: Never again will a woman have the leverage that will **motivate a man to change** towards Christ-likeness, like she has **before** marriage. Her ability to exercise her leverage will decrease in direct proportion to the time that has gone by since she met him. And there will be an even greater loss of leverage after they are married.

I can imagine that the very idea of telling a woman she has leverage over a man (or insinuating that she should use it) can rile some people. But please keep in mind that our goal with regards to her using leverage is that a man, be motivated to see his own needs and draw himself closer to God! Letting a woman know that she has that kind of leverage for those purposes shouldn't annoy a Christian. Especially when Scripture tells us to look for ways to motivate one another to Godliness. (Hebrews 10:24)

I'm reminded of a young lady who came to me one day because her boyfriend was already acting offensively and his ways were wounding her spirit. She wanted to know what she could do to get their relationship on the right track. I asked if she would be willing to require that he read my book, **Discovering the Mind of a Woman?**

"Oh, he wouldn't read it!" she objected.

I said, "I know of a way you could get him to read it." . . . (I'm getting ready to suggest that she use her leverage.)

She asked, "How?"

I replied, "Tell him you won't date him again until he reads it."

With alarm she said, "Ever again!? . . . What if he won't read it?!"

"You'll sure find out how serious he is about caring for you and building his relationship with the Lord, won't you? And wouldn't **now** be a better time to find that out than later?"

She thought for awhile. Then still struggling with reservations she decided, "I'll do it!" . . . (use her leverage).

Wednesday she offered him the book with her stipulations. **Friday** he asked her for a date.

"Have you read the book yet?" she challenged.

"No, but I will!" he assured her.

"Well, if you remember, I said I wouldn't go out with you again until **after** you've read it," she reminded him with determination.

When he saw she definitely was serious, he read it! It was the beginning of a new direction in their relationship and his relationship with the Lord. That book revealed a lot of concepts to him that this man wanted to develop in his life. He is letting me have the joy of discipling him. Working with them has been a great source of blessing to me. But all that happened because she was willing to use her leverage **to motivate him to have within himself a greater** concern for godliness. Is that so terrible?

My daughters have witnessed a great deal of grief in marriages. They've seen the results of men who do not know how to be the spiritual leaders. They've also seen the effects upon wives **who didn't pay attention before marriage** to the signs that reveal a man who could care less about anyone, other than himself. They want me to meet and get to know the guys they are about to date **before** they seriously date them. The guys are aware that I want to meet them because the girls have let them know that's how we operate. Some of the guys are very nervous; some take it in stride. As time goes on, as they hang around, these men develop an understanding of my perspective on marriage. If things start looking serious, I discuss with them what I see, concerning men, and the scriptural requirements in a marriage relationship.

Our first daughter, Denise was married in 1984. Her husband, Tim. became aware long before marrying her that a good relationship would require that they be honest with one another. Ever since our daughters were little girls, I've always said to them, "I'm only looking for one thing in the guys you date, as you might consider marriage. I'm not watching to see if he won the 'Christian of the Year' award, or if he's memorized the Bible, etc. I've seen too many marriages fall apart where the women were supposed to have married those 'wonderful' Christian men. I've seen only one quality that seems to make a significant difference in Christian men ... what I want for each of my daughters is a man who has a teachable spirit!" And Tim has not only illustrated that he has a good learner's spirit, he is also the source of a lot of joy to me while we are involved in his discipleship. I feel like he and I are best of friends; his friendship means a lot to me.

ALREADY MARRIED?

But let's say that your marriage didn't start off with a very good beginning. What can you do now? You can still be honest! But remember to be cautious and constructive with your honesty. **Don't try to kill.** Also, because you want to persuade him, don't condition your husband to **not** believe you by exaggerating your report.

Even though they want to be honest, many women make emotionally charged statements while under stress which tend to make their husbands discredit their trustworthiness. The tendency in men to misunderstand makes those statements appear as though they are specifically design- ed to **scare** a husband into action. For example, after many months, years, etc., a wife feels that her tolerance level has been reached due to her husband's attitudes of insensitivity—his insults, his verbal attacks, etc. So one day she decides she's got to let him know she's "had it!" She complains, "I can't take this kind of treatment anymore!" She intends that he hear her saying . . . If you don't stop it **I've gotta' get outa here** . . . but he doesn't recognize that that's what she means. (Remember, he's insensitive!) She thinks that because he has ears that are able to hear, he **understands** what she means. But hearing and understand- ing are two different things. Her husband thinks she's just a frequently fussy woman. This causes him to conclude that she's just an emotional mess—that's why she's always over- reacting. So he ignores her and their life-style continues on, "business as usual."

On another occasion, during another argument, he again belittles her. She says, "If I'm so unimportant to you, why do you stick around?" She intended that he hear . . . we're so miserable together, it seems like the only solution is that **somebody's gotta go!** Another time she says, "Are you try- ing to get rid of me; do you want **me** to leave?!" And another, "This has got to end!" And another, "I don't have to take this!" etc., etc. Gradually her threats get more severe, but he's also gradually getting more and more calloused to her threats. He could even think, "I'm really a big man because I've learned to tolerate all of her irrational emotional outbursts." He's heard all of this complaining before and yet life just keeps going on as usual!

Possibly friends of theirs hear his wife's threats and express concern. They question this husband about the seriousness of what they're hearing. The husband trys to reassure his friends. "Oh, she doesn't mean it! She's always saying things like that ... but she never does anything about it ... she'll get over it," he casually responds.

Then she leaves for a day to get his attention. He doesn't like the inconvenience of her being gone, so he promises to be good. He even does a couple of nice things to pacify her. He takes her out to dinner, buys her some flowers, etc., which seems to work. She has always wanted their marriage to work, so she lets him coax her back. In a very short time, though, it's back-to-the-same-old-stuff. So she takes off again, this time she leaves for a week or two. He assures her again that if she will come back things will be different. "That's what you said the last time," she complains. After a few more episodes of this I'll-change-if-you'll-come-back scenario, accompanied by the business-as-usual roller coaster ride, she leaves again. But he's convinced that this is still a part of her game and she'll be back. However, he is shocked when he discovers that this time something is different ... he gets divorce papers in the mail!!!

Can you see how always giving in and returning **before** a husband's character changes, can actually help condition a husband into believing, "It's not really all that serious ... she doesn't really mean it." Remember, men reflect and operate based on the mechanics of what's happening. They don't easily identify with a woman's emotions.

So please, if you don't mean them, don't say things just for effect! Don't throw away your "pry-bar" by saying things you don't really mean. There is also little value in saying things that do not have clear meaning **to him.** Remember most men operate simply on the meaning of words, not even considering the emotions behind those words—which might have motivated the words.

Please don't **wait until you really can't stand him anymore** and then take drastic measures serious enough to impress him with your emotional condition. You could be creating problems for yourself. If you wait until you're emotionally ready to die before trying to escape (taking a little "vacation" from him), the idea of returning to the "combat zone" becomes even more distasteful. The great contrast between the peace of being away from him, and the conflicts from being around him, will become more noticeable. You might lose all commitment to your marriage, and that's not good or right. So by **waiting until you hate him** and what he's doing so much that you just want to get out, you both lose! You might find yourself beyond caring whether you ever "wake him up" with drastic measures or anything else.

SECOND MARRIAGES

Then there's the compounded problems created by second marriages.

> Even though a man divorced his wife (or was divorced by his wife), it is amazing to see how many women actually believe the "new guy" when he says, "It was **all** my ex-wife's fault." I would like to ask you some simple questions. Would you leave a perfect husband? Wouldn't you instead, respond in gratefulness to a thoughtful, kind, loving husband? Wouldn't you be forever his if he were as wonderful to you as this man is trying to tell you he was to his former wife? Or would you try to offend him until he left you as he's trying to convince you she was foolish enough to do? Sure, he may seem charming and wonderful now ... but remember he was charming and wonderful before his marriage to another woman too. Surely you don't think he won her over with offensiveness.

There are many of you who have married or remarried and have discovered that your new husband, who was also divorced, doesn't know anything more about being your spiritual leader than he did for his first wife. There is something **very important** you both will need to realize now, before real solutions can be achieved. Whether or not he likes it, not only does he have **the responsibility** of caring for your emotional condition **in this present relationship,** but he also has **the responsibility** of caring for the condition of your spirit **caused by the damage from your previous marriage.** Does he know this? Is he prepared for all that responsibility?

> Please note that I am saying, RESPONSIBILITY FOR ... not BLAME FOR.

What's the future going to look like for this marriage if you don't learn to be constructively honest about the way you are being affected by negative conditions in your relationship with your new husband? If you were married before, what were the benefits in your last marriage from not being **constructively** honest?

Here's another problem that needs to be addressed:

After divorcing, a lot of those women start dating other men. Seeing an ex-wife dating will make many former husbands very desperate. Some will start "chasing" their ex-wife. And that puzzles many women. A wife might say, "Why are you interested now? When you had me you didn't care. Forget me! Find another woman! Start building another life! Leave me alone!"

Why are these husbands, all of a sudden, pursuing their wives?

TWO REASONS:

First, unfortunately, these husband's have **just become aware** (in many cases), that they've **really** had problems in their marriage.

Second, remember, I said men with problems are challenged to solve them. These separated husbands all of a sudden realize that their wives are **not theirs** anymore. Discovering that what he thought was his, is no longer his, challenges a man. It reactivates his conquering or problem solving instincts.

If your man is serious about winning you back, and at this point you can be sure he is, why not use that as leverage? Why not let the challenge to have you back serve the purpose of motivating him to make **lasting** changes in his character? Why shouldn't you utilize his instinctive desire to solve problems? Let **him** learn to work hard at building Christ-likeness in his life, creating the kind of relationship you've always wanted. Often men will try to **pressure** their wife into getting back together sooner— according to **his** time schedule. But that type of pressure reveals that additional changes are needed in his character. You will need to be **strong** and **honest** about your convictions. Insist that the significant changes God wants to see, and that you are looking for in him and in your relationship, become permanent **before** you take him back!

There **are** husbands who are working hard at becoming more Christ-like and rebuilding their marriage. They **do** want to learn how they've failed so they can change. I've told some wives who are resistant to reconsidering and getting back together with their husbands, "He **is** going to change and become the man/husband that he should have been all along. With that positive type of change in mind— after you've paid the price for him to finally wake up and come to this point of desperation (wanting to change his character)—are you still going to dump him? Now that he's finally willing to make permanent changes, are you going to let some other woman possibly reap the rewards of your agony? Are you going to let some other woman have the joy of a rewarding relationship with **your** husband?"

Once a husband is in the process of changing, and he is trying hard, he may, as a "natural" reponse to relationship pressures, unconsciously try to persuade his wife to give him a break and go light on pointing out problem areas. Help him see the lack of commitment in that attitude, too. Let him know you're troubled when he wants you to "back off", because to give in to him would make you both irresponsible. Actually he is trying to pressure you into yielding to his old nature. It would be better for him if he would measure his own progress, by watching, to see how you **respond to** Christ-likeness in his life. Let him know that as he becomes more Christ-like, you will be more inclined to trust him and want to be near him. He may try to convince you that he'll lose his determination if you don't give in to his timetable! Again, remind him that that kind of statement makes you question the strength and length of his commitment. Let him know that you need to see that his motivation to change is based on **his commitment** to become Christ-like. You want him to prove to you, that any changes are not designed **just** with the purpose of influencing you into returning to him. Remind him that part of your past frustration was centered, mainly, around his lacking the goal of Christ-likeness in his own life; it was not his top priority and motivation. To a great extent that's what caused **you** to lose hope and give up. Be constructively honest!

If you hear warnings from others about negative characteristics in the man you are planning to marry, be prompt to examine their claims. It won't hurt you to further validate his character; and let's hope he won't mind proving himself and the validity of his desire to become, as your spiritual leader, more and more Christ-like. Don't let it be said of you, "Nobody could tell me!"

CHAPTER TWELVE

SEVEN MYSTERIES SOLVED

Here are seven miscellaneous situations that plague most marriages and need to be cleared up.

SPECIAL EVENTS

Have you ever wondered why some wives seem to always remember special occasions and remember to get gifts and yet it's so hard for men to remember these things? Well, aside from the fact that wives are naturally inclined and then especially alert to the things that are important to relationships, a wife's normal household responsibilities (such as shopping), put her right in the middle of the type of surroundings which prompt reminders of gift-giving. Being around card racks, gift stores, craft shops, etc., is an almost everyday occurrence to wives. Husbands mostly go from home to work and back. They seldom have a habit of browsing around in stores. So they are at a disadvantage when it comes to having reminders about special occasions. This is not to excuse men, though. Men still need to learn more about remembering special occasions and being thoughtful about remembering gifts, because that helps them prove how much they care about those they love. A wife's reminders to her husband about special occasions can be very helpful.

LOVE AND SICKNESS

Here's another common occurrence:

Your husband must really be sick—so sick, that he stayed home from work and went to bed. During the morning, because you love him and care about him, you go into the bedroom to check on him. He's awakened, so you ask him if there's anything you can do for him. He moans, "No, just let me sleep." Later on, you find yourself tenderly thinking about him so you check in on him again. Once more he wakes up. "Anything I can do for you?" you lovingly ask. Impatiently he complains, "No, **please,** just let me sleep!" More time goes by and he hasn't eaten anything all day. That evening, out of concern, you decide to find out if there is anything he would like. When you go into the room, you awake him to see if he would like anything. He snaps back, "Yes, as a matter of fact, there is . . . I would like for you to leave me alone, stop bothering me, and let me sleep!" You feel hurt and offended, but you try to make excuses for him by telling yourself that he's acting like that because he's sick. But you can't make that hold water because you think, if a buddy were to come over to check on him, he wouldn't treat his buddy like that.

So why should he treat you like that, when you're just trying to lovingly care for him. Why is it, that men don't seem to want attention at times like that? Well, in a lot of cases, when a man is sick he just wants to be left alone in his misery . . . to die or sleep, whichever. That's just how a lot of men respond when they're really feeling bad.

Now, on the other hand, when you get sick and by noon nobody has been in to check on you, you start feeling neglected. (And anyone who really cares would know to check on you, wouldn't they?) And this is where the puzzle becomes more puzzling. All day he has left you alone. He even keeps the kids away; he doesn't want them to go in and bother you either. By evening, you're feeling so unloved and uncared for that you drag yourself out of bed, wander out to where the family is and longingly ask, "Why didn't anyone even come in to check on me? None of you cares if I live or die, do you?" Your husband is flabbergasted! He responds, "When I was sick all I wanted to do was sleep, but you wouldn't let me! So I figured **I'd be nice to you** and let you alone, to sleep."

Even though a husband's response to his wife's sickness may seem unsympathetic and look like he doesn't care, that isn't always true. Often in a husband's confusion, he just doesn't know how to express his caring in a way with which his wife **can identify.** Maybe this illustration will prompt you to discuss with each other how you would like to be cared for when you're sick.

HIDDEN LIVES

Here's another problem that further complicates meaningful relationships. There are some women who never let their feelings be known. The reasons can be many: parental abuse, feelings of inferiority, a timid nature, thinking silence in a marriage is equal to spiritual maturity, etc. But if women don't let their husbands know what their feelings are, chances are a husband may never discover what his wife's true feelings are. Which will make it impossible for him to care for her needs.

If it's difficult for you to put your feelings into words, get help. If you can, get help through lay counselors or get professional help, it's worth it. Don't live your life in secret, within yourself. (If for no other reason than that you may, because of your refusal to get help, pass on to your children the inability to see what is involved in successfully communicating.)

DON'T JUDGE A BOOK BY ITS COVER

This is another **serious** concern. One of the biggest problems in marriages today is that too many women were attracted to their husband because of surface attractions and thought that was "falling in love." I sure wish more women would be guided by spiritually significant reasons, rather than just surface attractions, when they're considering a man for marriage. A man may **appear** wonderful, but as you spend time with him, have you discovered whether or not he has a serious commitment to be obedient to God? Has he ever made you feel pressured to lower your standards, ignoring your resistance. Is he motivated by his own selfish reasons or desires? Does he seek to **honor you** as Christ would? There's too much at stake to pass up the seriousness of these questions.

FALSE IMAGES

Speaking of surface attractions, let me emphasize another problem in the Christian community. Many Christians have observed an individual's public conduct or, noticed that many people were attracted to that person. These Christians then, determine that this person they admire is a good or powerfully spiritual person, and then these same Christians set out to make themselves into a duplicate of that individual. But Scripture says:

> *"For we dare not make ourselves of the number, or compare ourselves with some that commend*

themselves; but they, measuring themselves by themselves, and comparing themselves among themselves, are not wise." (II Cor. 10:12 KJV)

A serious flaw in trying to duplicate others is this: We lose sight of the fact that Christ is to be our example. Our only requirement as a Christian, is to become like Him. Instead, many people put effort into becoming like the individual they admire. And there are too many individuals in positions of leadership who are willing to let searching Christians follow them instead of emphatically directing those who are searching to Christ. So let me exhort you to make Christ your example. Not men! If you see a "good Christian" and that person allows you to think they "have it together" because they never acknowledge to you or anyone else that they have shortcomings ... beware!

TRUE REPENTANCE

I have heard many wives who refuse to believe that their husband is genuinely repentant. They tend to measure his repentance with their own experience of repentance. These wives usually say, "If he were really repentant he would have _____!"
But if we are all unique before God, then we will all respond to life differently. We will even respond differently year by year if we are growing as a Christian. If a wife has a keener capacity to identify with emotions than her husband has, then she will naturally respond with more grief, tears, remorse, etc., when she experiences repentance. But most husbands are not nearly as able to identify with emotions as their wives are. So they naturally will not be as emotional when they experience repentance. As they become more and more like Christ, they will become more able to experience emotions. Then you might see more grief, tears, remorse, etc. But no one should judge the sincerity of another person's repentance; comparing it to their own emotional capacity.

It's not unusual for a wife to say, "When I hurt him, and ask him to forgive me, I feel terrible. When he hurts me, and he asks me to forgive him, he doesn't seem to feel anything." Although the comparison of the differences in feelings is legitimate, to judge the sincerity of his desire to reconcile by his capacity to experience sorrow is not legitimate.

I'm grateful when a husband comes to the point where he is willing to believe that emotions are legitimate; and that those emotions can be proof that a person has a spirit; and that he is, more and more, able to experience the reality of his own spirit; and that a spirit can be hurt; and that he believes his wife's spirit has been hurt; and that he cares, even though he has much to learn about what it means, to more effectively identify with the spirit of another person. We've got to be patient while God accomplishes, little by little, what men have been spending a lifetime avoiding or resisting or missing.

HEALING

Christ is the great physician. And I believe a husband is to be Christ's representative in his marriage. Of course, the more a man's ego is surrenderd to Christ, the more that man's body will be activated by Christ in him. If he is not surrendered to Christ, he will not be "as" Christ. If he is not committed to being "as" Christ he does not have the authority of Christ. "As" Christ, a husband **will be** able to minister to his wife's spirit—and the spirit of their relationship **will be** healthy and lovingly vibrant even if his wife's physical health is failing.

Discovering the damage he has caused, many a husband has asked me what he can do to heal his wife. It is important to realize that when it comes to life, the natural tendency for every life form is to set about repairing itself, to restore itself, to be healed. Even the human spirit seeks to heal itself. The key is to **stop the damage.** Relationship healing is hindered only by continued damage. Stop the wounding and in most cases the natural by-product is healing.

IN CONCLUSION

It is our prayer that this book will be helpful in turning the tide of divorce. We would love to have a part in seeing unhappy, unfulfilled marriage relationships turned around and see new marriages start out right—Christ-centered. It is our desire that Christian marriages will be a light in the world, showing the world the right way to build relationships. How great it would be if more husbands would learn how to make the change from 'normal' men into Christlike, Christian men; as even **their wives would testify.**

If this book has helped you, I am grateful. Maybe you feel there are some valid points in here that you would like your husband to examine because they represent conditions in your marriage. Maybe you could ask him to read it too. But don't forget, most men are not likely to read it just because **you asked him.** You will need to present it to him as a challenge! If your husband needs a challenge, here's what I would suggest. I would get one of those little yellow pads with the stick-um on the back. Then I would write a note to him and stick it on the cover of this book. This is what it would say, "I've highlighted all the things in this book that I think relate to our marriage. I don't know for sure how you will handle finding out what I've highlighted? Not many men can read something this serious all the way through and respond maturely too. Will you be able to?

Don't forget your God-given role to be a constructive helper . . . you'll be helping God, too.

God Bless!

☐ I would like to receive _____ additional copies of this book, **Discovering the Heart of a Man,** at $7.95 a copy.

☐ I would like to receive _____ copies of the book, **Discovering the Mind of a Woman,** at $6.95 a copy.

I am enclosing $_____ to cover expenses. (Please include $1.00 a book for postage and handling.)

Note: All copies of Discovering the Heart of a Man sold within the state of Arizona must include a 6½ percent sales tax (.52 each).

NAME _____

ADDRESS _____

CITY _____ STATE _____ ZIP _____

Cut out and mail to:

Ken Nair
3513 E. Onyx Avenue
Phoenix, Arizona 85028

☐ I would like to receive _____ additional copies of this book, **Discovering the Heart of a Man,** at $7.95 a copy.

☐ I would like to receive _____ copies of the book, **Discovering the Mind of a Woman,** at $6.95 a copy.

I am enclosing $_____ to cover expenses. (Please include $1.00 a book for postage and handling.)

Note: All copies of Discovering the Heart of a Man sold within the state of Arizona must include a 6½ percent sales tax (.52 each).

NAME _____

ADDRESS _____

CITY _____ STATE _____ ZIP _____

Cut out and mail to:

Ken Nair
3513 E. Onyx Avenue
Phoenix, Arizona 85028